Praise for *Shining Li*

"On every page Wiens reveals where ... find God. It isn't easy. It's really simple. Exactly."

—Jon M. Sweeney, coauthor,
Meister Eckhart's Book of the Heart

"If you miss the childlike wonder that once intuited there was more to life than meets the eye, commune with these pages and you just might find your soul."

—Phileena Heuertz, founding partner, Gravity, a Center for Contemplative Activism; author of *Pilgrimage of a Soul: Contemplative Spirituality for the Active Life* and *Mindful Silence: The Heart of Christian Contemplation*

"Wiens circles round questions that have intrigued people for millennia: Where am I? What is God? How do I love? He takes his faith as seriously as his doubt, and offers practices that exercise both body and belief."

—Pádraig Ó Tuama, author of *In the Shelter*; inaugural poet laureate of The On Being Project

"Wiens winsomely guides readers through a collection of time-tested spiritual practices that will ground them in the present moment and grow their awareness of God's loving presence."

—Ed Cyzewski, author of *Flee, Be Silent, Pray* and *Reconnect: Spiritual Restoration from Digital Distraction*

"In a world where it seems everyone is deconstructing faith, it's refreshing to read a book about rekindling faith. Trust the guidance of Steve Wiens as he offers an invitation to practices that will lead you to communion with the divine. *Shining Like the Sun* takes us on a journey of rediscovering the God of the Bible. You will find Steve Wiens to be a compassionate guide to bring clarity and gentle encouragement."

—Karen Gonzalez, author of *The God Who Sees*

"I have followed Steve Wiens for a long time, and he has never failed to open my eyes to things I have missed, things right there in front of me. When I read his book *Whole*, I followed him into the idea that I could find myself in many places in Scripture. When I listen to his podcast, I follow him into new ideas of faith and love and stillness. I would follow Steve Wiens anywhere. In *Shining Like the Sun*, he asks us to follow him on a search for God. Sign me up."

—Shawn Smucker, author of *Light from Distant Stars*

SHINING LIKE THE SUN

SHINING LIKE THE SUN

*Seven Mindful Practices for
Rekindling Your Faith*

STEVE WIENS

Fortress Press

Minneapolis

SHINING LIKE THE SUN
Seven Mindful Practices for Rekindling Your Faith

Cover design: Kevin van der Leek

Print ISBN: 978-1-5064-5666-9
eBook ISBN: 978-1-5064-5667-6

CONTENTS

If faith is a high-flying circus act
the biggest moments happen after you've
let go of one trapeze
but before you've grabbed the
other.

It may be terrifying to hang there
in between those two horizontal bars
but how can you resist
swinging even farther
now?

This book is for anyone who wants to learn
to love that moment between
letting go and grabbing hold.

Finding God Where You Are

Well, here you are, reading a book about rekindling your faith, for God's sake, despite the fact that you've long since lost the scent, despite the church and its foul theology, despite your worn-out eureka moments having long since expired. Maybe the only thing you know for sure is that some essential *something* has gone missing, and you're willing to look anywhere to find it. You keep trying to find God because there really are things you still want from God, and that desire is perhaps the most glorious thing about you.

Question: Where are you looking?

There's an ancient story in which God, having recently created human beings, realized that a terrible mistake had been made. After calling the elders together, God explained, "I have just created humans, and now I don't know what

I'm going to do. They will always be talking to me, and wanting things from me, and I won't ever get any rest." The elders furrowed their brows. One by one, they all agreed: God had a very big problem indeed. They suggested God could hide on Mount Everest, or the moon, or even deep inside the earth.

"No," God said. "Humans are resourceful; eventually they will find me there." After a very long silence, one elder whispered something in God's ear. "That's it!" God shouted, smiling. "I'll hide inside of each human; they will never find me there!"

The punchline is obvious: we look for God everywhere except inside ourselves. And why would we? The journey within is troubling enough without wondering if we'll find God-as-Mary-Poppins, dragging our dirty laundry out of its hiding places (*spit-spot!*), or worse, that we'll find a kind but clear breakup letter left on the pillow *(it's not you, it's me)*. And anyway, you've most likely already found and lost God more than once. For all we know, our search for God may have been responsible for the finding and also for the losing.

But what if it's not a joke? What if God really is hidden inside us?

Maybe it feels absurd, naïve, and overly self-referential to even indulge that question. If we look deep within ourselves, whatever is down there must be unbearably shy because it only seems to poke its head out when we grieve a terrible loss or taste the emptiness of success—or when we realize someone genuinely likes us. Indulging that question can feel a little too much like a riddle when we're looking for answers. I hate riddles. It takes a dozen or so wrong answers before you finally get the right one. I hate how the wrong answers clutter up the space we need to figure out the right answer. But I also love riddles. I love that laugh-out-loud moment of pure joy when the answer pops into your head, when you realize you were making it so much harder than it needed to be.

And isn't it the absurdity of a God who would hide within humans at least part of what keeps us looking in the first place? It's wildly unreasonable to expect we'll find what we're looking for, but humans are notorious suckers for wildly unreasonable quests (*a few of my favorite suckers include Sir Ernest Shackleton, Mary Shelley, Mahatma Gandhi, Jean Vanier, Martin Luther King Jr., and the Virgin Mary*). Maybe it's naïve to assume God even cares about what we want, but a little naïveté doesn't mean our deepest desires are weightless things that float around in a zero-gravity chamber until someone packs them away again.

Finally, a brief word about this wildly unreasonable quest: it's not a scavenger hunt and we aren't looking for a needle in a haystack. There will be no searching for the face of Jesus on a tortilla. Paradoxically, this quest won't require us to find *anything*. We're going to need to pay careful attention to where we *are* instead of overfocusing on where we are *going*. We're going to see haystacks as great places to take naps, and we're going to let the needles find themselves. We're going to get stuck in certain places and feel tempted to leave before we should. We're going to be tempted to avoid certain places where we really need to linger. We're going to end up in places that seem like no place at all.

> Paradoxically, this quest won't require us to find *anything*. We're going to need to pay careful attention to where we *are* instead of overfocusing on where we are *going*. ●

Let the rekindling begin! God help us all.

There is a way to search for God that doesn't rekindle faith as much as it rekindles busyness and behavior modification. That kind of journey, with all its earnestness and urgency, burns people out. Let's not go there. There's also a way to search for God that's so angry at the fire you grew up with that you never do anything other than deconstruct the *idea* of fire. That kind of journey is fun at first, until you realize you're just walking in circles. Let's not go there, either. But then are you left searching for a God so ambiguous and nameless that you have to *pretend* you're sitting around a fire even though everybody is freezing to death? There must be another way to search for God.

It drove most people crazy, but Jesus talked about finding God using mostly paradoxical language, like needing to lose your life if you want to find it, needing to hate your family if you want to be worthy of following him, and selling the farm to buy a field with hidden treasure buried ten paces west of the big oak tree. Paradox resists formulas and always makes room for mystery. The kind of faith that I believe needs rekindling is paradoxical in nature; it grows by getting pared down, and it gets strengthened by embracing the weakest parts.

Meister Eckhart, the thirteenth-century Christian mystic whose writings influenced Thomas Merton, Richard Rohr, and many other mystical/guru types, never met a paradox he didn't like. He cautioned that those who seek God through a specific kind of "way" might end up with the way but won't end up with God. Eckhart once said, "Ours is the task of learning to seek God 'without a way' and 'without a why,' meaning to open ourselves to the surprising and often unsettling adventure that constitutes the search."

In *Meister Eckhart's Book of the Heart: Meditations for the Restless Soul,* Jon Sweeney and Mark Burrows have taken Meister Eckhart's dense teaching and translated it into some of the most gorgeous poetry I've ever read. I carry their little book with me everywhere I go. The following poem from that book describes a paradoxical search for God that I find irresistible:

Here and Now

Everything hangs on the little word
here and its sibling *now*, but I often

forget this, keeping busy with my
plans, building for a future I cannot

know and against worries I cannot
finally tame, and yet You wait

for me to come home to Your now
which is beyond past and future,

and return to Your here which is
present before beginning and

beyond every ending.

The "wayless way" of searching for God shares similarities with mindfulness and seems to be consistent with how Jesus thought about searching for God. Eckhart's wayless way calls us, again and again and again, to quietly return to a place called Here, where God is eternally waiting for us with love in a moment called Now. If we can return to Here as we unload the dishwasher, we might notice the simple beauty of a piece of handmade pottery, which might eventually help us notice all the beauty not made by human hands. If we can fully receive a hug from a good friend, we might also be able to fully receive a surprising touch from the Divine. If we learn to fully enjoy each sip of coffee in the morning, we might also fully enjoy the million or so other good gifts God hides everywhere.

If we can return to Here in a season of pain and loss, maybe we can even be resurrected. A story is told about a time Saint Francis of Assisi couldn't find God anywhere. Exasperated, he found himself alone with an almond tree in the middle of winter. "Brother Almond, speak to me of God," he begged its bare branches. The dormant almond tree immediately responded by bursting into bloom.

Practicing mindfulness by returning to Here allows us to see each moment as a place where God is eternally waiting for us with love. Read that sentence again. If that all sounds a little too *woo-woo*, and if you're starting to hear the soft banjo and the airy NPR voice right now, allow me to intro- duce you to the mindfulness hidden within ancient biblical Hebrew, with all its sex and violence and treachery (*and very little banjo*).

In biblical Hebrew, the word for place is *hamakom* (*inci- dentally, biblical Hebrew doesn't contain vowels, so that's a transliteration*). *Hamakom* stems from the root word *kum*, which means to stand. A place is where you stand or where you remain. In rabbinic literature, it is assumed that God is not only the transcendent Master of the Universe, but also the immanently present ground upon which one stands in each and every moment. In fact, God is often referred to as *Hama-kom*. If God is the place where you stand, this very moment contains the entire cosmos. And if God is every place you stand, you carry the cosmos with you wherever you go. It turns out mindfulness is baked into one of the names for God.

Take this brief, ancient example. The first book of the Hebrew Bible is Genesis, which turns out to mostly be about brothers trying to kill each other. Cain murdered Abel after God didn't like his sacrifice, Joseph's brothers left him for dead at the bottom of a dried-out cistern, and Esau hunted his twin brother Jacob down like a dog after Jacob swindled him out of a birthright and a blessing. I have twin boys, so I know twin swindling. Let's camp there for a bit.

In the story of Esau and Jacob, we read that when they were born, Esau came out of Rebecca's womb first, his tiny body apparently covered in a thick blanket of red hair. When Jacob slid out next, his fist was wrapped tightly around Esau's heel, as if to say, "Not so fast, buddy." As they grew up, Esau and Jacob were opposites. Esau enjoyed the simple pleasures of a bowl of stew after a day out hunting with his father, but Jacob was always hungry for what he didn't have. It's complicated, but Esau accepted Jacob's manipulative offer of a bowl of his famous stew in exchange for his birthright. Just wait, it gets worse.

Jacob also stole the blessing meant for the firstborn, which would have secured Esau's future, by gluing some hair on his arms and hoodwinking their father Isaac—who was blind as a bat—into blessing him instead. These two events left Esau starved of a future that was rightly his, while Jacob ended up with a belly full of hope. Before the dust of those decisions settled, Jacob was on his way to his uncle's house to get himself a wife from among his cousins. A quick recap of Genesis so far: blood, murder, treachery, and now incest! How in the world is this searching for God?

Jacob's faith was rekindled when he fell asleep.

> But on the way to that place, [Jacob] came to a certain place [Hebrew: *hamakom*] and stayed there for the night, because the sun had set. Taking one of the stones of the place [*hamakom*], he put it under his head and lay down in that place [*hamakom*]. (Gen 28:11 (NRSV)

The Hebrew Scriptures were written with a gauzy subtlety, which can sometimes border on subterfuge. Those who learn to pay attention to the small things often discover what others pass right over—small things like repeating a word three times in one verse. When *hamakom* is repeated, it's a hint that you need to start asking some questions. What—*not where*—was this certain place? Although Jacob got everything he wanted, what did he still lack? What happened when the sun set?

In Jewish culture, a day doesn't begin at sunrise; it begins when you can see the first few twinkling stars after the sun has gone down. At the beginning of this new day, with ten thousand yesterdays behind him and a million tomorrows ahead, Jacob fell asleep. He dreamed of a ladder on which angels climbed up and down, above which God stood and spoke to Jacob: "I am the God of your father and his father," God tells Jacob, "and I will bless you with many descendants."

Even if the twinkling stars tell you today is over, you haven't yet arrived at tomorrow if you know exactly what it's going to hold; if you know, you're stuck in yesterday. You're not at the beginning of a brand-new day if you think you can see everything you need to see and if you think you know everything there is to know. I warned you the Bible sometimes borders on subterfuge.

God, it turns out, wasn't finished speaking to Jacob: "I will be with you and keep you wherever you go and will bring you back to this land; for I will not leave you until I have done what I have promised you" (Gen. 28:15 NRSV) This is Jacob's moment of returning to Here and finding God waiting for him in that Now. This is what finally snapped Jacob out of his lifelong slumber. This is Jacob's laugh-out-loud moment of pure joy. Stealing his brother's birthright and blessing had been absurdly self-referential, and it was naïve to believe that a false blessing sending him to a new place would launch him into a true future. Rather, God's words were the blessing Jacob had been searching for all along, and he was aware and awake enough to receive it, even though he was paradoxically asleep when it was offered to him. The effect of his father's blindness was reversed when he found himself standing in the place of being seen by God. The pain of his twin brother's otherness was healed by touching the reality of union with God so deeply that he knew he would never be alone again. When Jacob woke up from his dream in that certain place, a foundational shift had taken place. When he realized where he really was, for the first time in his life, he didn't want to go anywhere else. He was *within* God.

Jacob said, "Surely the Lord was in this place [*hama-kom*], and I was not aware of it." In that moment, Jacob was the almond tree that burst into bloom. For Jacob to wake up, he needed to fall asleep. Notice how Jacob tells the story of his moment of transformation. By saying the Lord "was in this place" (*past tense*) and he "was not aware of it" (*past tense*), he's telling us we will find the Lord in this Now (*present tense*) if we can simply return to this Here (*present tense*).

When you can return to Here, you can come alive to the reality that God is found there, wherever there is. When you touch life deeply in each moment, you come alive to the reality that the entire cosmos is contained in this very moment. We'll get where we need to go when we learn to be where we are. It's how the way of mindfulness is made.

> We'll get where we need to go when we learn to be where we are. 🔹

Can you stand in a place long enough to see where you really are?

Can you stand in a place long enough to see who is there with you?

Can you stand in a place long enough to see you don't need to go anywhere else?

The way of mindfulness is gentle, like falling asleep and waking up. Its slow and steady work is marked by increasing levels of wonder in ordinary moments, enabling you to be present and at one with those around you and with what you are doing.

Another brief example of paying attention to the moment is one that doesn't include any treachery or blood or incest or stew. One day, the modern mystic Thomas Merton was out running errands in *a Certain Place*—the intersection of Fourth and Walnut in Louisville, Kentucky—when he became aware and awake to where he really was. As Merton wrote later,

> I was suddenly overwhelmed with the realization that I loved all those people, that they were mine and I theirs, that we could not be alien to one another even though we were total strangers. It was like waking from a dream of separateness, of spurious self-isolation in a special world, the world of renunciation and supposed holiness. . . . This sense of liberation from an illusory difference was such a relief and such a joy to me that I

almost laughed out loud. . . . I have the immense joy of being man, a member of a race in which God Himself became incarnate. As if the sorrows and stupidities of the human condition could overwhelm me, now I realize what we all are. And if only everybody could realize this! But it cannot be explained. There is no way of telling people that they are all walking around shining like the sun. Then it was as if I suddenly saw the secret beauty of their hearts, the depths of their hearts where neither sin nor desire nor self-knowledge can reach, the core of their reality, the person that each one is in God's eyes. If only they could all see themselves as they really are. If only we could see each other that way all the time. There would be no more war, no more hatred, no more cruelty, no more greed. But this cannot be seen, only believed and "understood" by a peculiar gift.

Merton found God where he found himself, which also happened to be where he found everybody else. By writing about his experience, he indulges in a little biblical subterfuge himself: he knows that the only way to get people to embark on a journey to discover they are shining like the sun is to tell them he can't tell them about it. Thomas Merton may have been brilliant, but he wasn't a unicorn. That moment on Fourth and Walnut "suddenly" came after years of deep pain and loss when silence was his only companion.

For some of us, it may take a similar childlike wonder for us to believe there is a place in the depth of our hearts where our secret beauty shines like the sun. For others, it may require indulging in naïveté, or agreeing to go on a wildly unreasonable quest, or giving in to some carefully planned subterfuge. If you engage in a mindful search for God by learning to become aware and awake to where you are, you will find a peculiar gift waiting for you.

You and I are like Saint Francis, begging someone to speak to us of God. He asked and was given an almond tree in bloom. I offer you seven metaphorical almond trees— seven mindful practices that show us how to truly come alive in various ways:

1. To become aware and awake to the present moment, I practice *attentiveness.*
2. To return to who I am, I practice *ordinariness.*
3. To touch life deeply in every moment of daily life, I practice *simplicity.*
4. To live in harmony with those around me, I practice *rhythm.*
5. To be present with those I consider "other," I practice *conversation.*
6. To be truly alive with what I am doing, I practice *delight.*
7. To be at one with all of creation, I practice *restoration.*

As you engage with these mindful practices in your own unique way, I hope you experience deep levels of joy and freedom. I hope you grow in self-compassion and in love for others. I hope you experience the surprising nearness of God in ways that wake you up to the possibility of human flourishing. I hope you come to love the moment of letting go as much as you come to love the moment of grabbing hold. And I hope you see yourself shining like the sun.

*   *   ●   *   *

Ever Shining Light

Some days it seems the whole world
is tilting the wrong way: it might be up

but I am somehow down, and right is
always somewhere against my

wrong, and then You remind me that
within me burns an ever shining light

which no night or stumbling down
can ever fully dim or finally smite.

Attentiveness

To become aware and awake to the present moment, I
practice attentiveness: learning to return to Here so I can
find God waiting for me with love in the eternal Now.

Can you tell me when you're going to be done with whatever you're doing on your phone, so we can finish our
conversation?"

I remain convinced that I can engage in a conversation
while also scrolling through Twitter, but my wife, Mary,
doesn't believe me. And anyway, how rude! Who starts a
conversation with someone whose face is down and whose
thumbs are busy? Granted, it's possible that she started the
conversation before I absentmindedly pulled out my phone
and started scrolling, but I guess we'll never know.

If we don't stay in touch with our desire to return to Here, it's easy to lose sight of the important people and events in our lives. Using the metaphor of a person trapped inside a phone booth while frantically swatting at a bee, Martin Laird calls this way of responding to the world "the reactive mind," a state of being unable to settle into Here or Now and being overwhelmed with distractions. Rather than attending to what's in front of us, the reactive mind is always focused on what's missing, convinced life would be instantly better if we could just get our hands on it, whatever it is. Scrolling through Twitter isn't necessarily bad (*how else will the world know how witty I am?*), unless I start believing Twitter has more to offer than a conversation with my wife.

As an alternative, Laird suggests cultivating a different state of mind, a receptive mind, by returning again and again and again to solitude and contemplative prayer. These are practices Thomas Merton spent a lifetime doing, which led to his transcendent experience on Fourth and Walnut in Louisville that I described earlier. I'll discuss those practices later, but first I'd like to explain why we resist them so much.

The brain is wired to stay reactive because it "thinks" being receptive is too dangerous. The same prehistoric part of our brains that tell us to gobble up as many Snickers bars as possible because they might only be in bloom for two weeks also tells us to run like hell from anything that's unfamiliar. If the receptive mind encourages us to linger in the

Here and Now so we can see what might emerge, the reactive mind tells us that's a great way to get killed. If we let our guard down and stop to enjoy those blueberries on our way home from a stressful day of hunting and gathering, a saber-toothed tiger might stop to enjoy us for dinner.

When the reactive mind isn't keeping us safe from getting killed, it's convincing us we're missing out on something good by lingering where we are. If I stop scrolling through Twitter to engage in a conversation with my wife, I might miss reading all the enthusiastic affirmations of my witty banter. If you swipe left on a Tinder bio that reads, "I like long walks on the beach with my girlfriend, until the LSD wears off and I realize I'm just dragging a stolen mannequin around a Wendy's parking lot," you might miss out on meeting the love of your life. If you go to bed early so you can have time to meditate in the morning, you might miss out "me time," that magical end of the day when you finally get to do what you want to do.

Rekindling your faith isn't just about learning to return to Here in the big, sacred moments of life. It's also about learning to return to Here in the very ordinary moments of life.

> Rekindling your faith isn't just about learning to return to Here in the big, sacred moments of life. It's also about learning to return to Here in the very ordinary moments of life. ●

• ◦ ● ◦ •

Practice: Returning to Here while Doing Ordinary Tasks

During a dinner I was having with some friends, someone asked, "What spiritual practices are you finding most helpful lately?" After a few tepid responses from the rest of us, a man in his sixties offered this: "Before I send an email, I close my eyes and picture the face of the person to whom I'm writing. I don't send the email until I've held their face in my imagination long enough to remember who they really are and what they mean to me."

What if we paused long enough to visualize the person's face and remember what they mean to us before pressing send? We'd cultivate a receptive mind, create space to experience gratitude, or even become aware of a resentment that might need to be addressed. We'd be returning to Here instead of just clearing out our inbox.

We can also practice returning to Here when we're getting things done around the house or in the yard. Instead of rushing through those tasks so we can finally relax later, we could open ourselves up to the possibility that a transcendent moment might be hiding just beneath the surface.

One autumn day while I was raking leaves, my son Ben called out from a corner of our backyard. "Come over here, daddy," he said. "Look!" The dry leaves crunched under my feet as I walked toward Ben. He was pointing at a plastic red rose, bright and beautiful, smiling at us from the other side of the fence. Someone had planted it behind a small pine sapling—easy to miss, unless you have Ben's eyes, which always seem to see what's hidden in plain sight. When I bent down to look at the rose, his eyes were shining. He was seeing way more than I was seeing. I think that plastic rose might actually have bloomed to life, but you'd have to ask Ben.

Who cares if the rose was fake? The story isn't about the rose. It's about returning to Here and seeing my son, who has way more to offer even than the satisfying feeling of getting a job done quickly.

When we stay in reactive mind, we'll only see and experience routine moments and familiar people as we've always seen and experienced them. We'll only make preprogrammed choices and have preprogrammed reactions. Practicing attentiveness begins with returning to Here so we can engage awareness in a new way. The moment we become aware we're missing what's in front of us because we're pining for something that's missing, we can return to Here by stopping to get curious about what's waiting for us Now. ●

● ● ◆ ● ●

Practice: Returning to Here by Abandoning Your Views

If God is eternally waiting for us with love in a moment called Now, a fake rose or an email is as good a place as any to learn to linger. But let's be honest. That phrase—"where God is eternally waiting for us with love"—can feel a bit off-putting if you've ever read the Bible. Although the Bible remains one of the most familiar places people still search for God, it also remains one of the hardest places to find God or to see anything new. It's hard to return to Here when you can't get past feeling triggered by one of the Bible's many confusing and sometimes contradictory passages. It's hard to return to Here when our serious questions about the Bible haven't been taken seriously enough.

Even though I've been a spiritual teacher and writer for twenty-five years, I admit it's hard to see how the Bible tells a story that love is stronger than anything else; it can seem like a collection of real curses and fake blessings. For a lot of us, the Bible became a house of cards that finally collapsed. Yet any robust conversation about rekindling our faith must at least address the reality that many of us need our faith in the Bible to be rekindled, even though that's a pretty tall order. Can the Bible really lead us to finding the God that is waiting for us with love in the eternal Now?

If we're willing to let go of the trapeze that got us here, we might have a chance to find that kind of God. If we're willing to live in that terrifying moment before we grab onto the next trapeze, we might even discover a mindful way to read the Bible. "For things to be revealed to us," Thich Nhat Hanh observed, "we need to be ready to abandon our views about them."

We can abandon the Bible altogether, or we can abandon a certain way of seeing the Bible. What if there was a way to see the contradictions in the Bible as a subversive device the writers intentionally included as a way to create space for people in every generation to ask their serious questions? What if there was a way to keep turning its familiar stories over and over until we can see new meanings that speak to new challenges? What if we stopped forcing the Bible to be divine historical journalism and started looking for the differences between *true* stories and *truth* stories? What if we let go of the trapeze by learning to ask the Bible some really hard questions, letting it squirm for a while before we accept its answers?

To get started, ask yourself this: How does the Bible talk about love?

Paradoxically, the first time the word *love* is mentioned in the Bible is when God tests a father by commanding him to murder his beloved son—that is, the one he loves. What's love got to do with murder? But if God really is loving, these gruesome stories have to bear the burden of proof.

The backstory: God promised Abram and his wife Sarai that they would begin a family through whom God would bless the whole world, but it took twenty years to have their first son. During those twenty years, they lost hope that God would fulfill that promise and tried to force it to happen on their own in every imaginable way. Reactive mind worked pretty well even back then.

The story: After Isaac was finally born, God "tests" Abraham by telling him to take his only son, Isaac—the one he *loves*—and sacrifice him as a burnt offering. We raise an eyebrow as Abraham agrees without question. We grimace as Abraham and Isaac walk three days into the middle of nowhere. We wince as they climb the mountain and prepare the altar. We stare in wide-eyed horror when Isaac sees the wood on the altar but doesn't see the sacrifice being prepared. When we see Abraham tie Isaac down and raise the knife, we want to throw up. What is happening? This is bad. This is very bad.

But just before the knife falls, with his chest still heaving and his heart still hammering, Abraham hears an angel tell him he has passed the test and that he is not to harm the boy. Abraham unties Isaac and instead sacrifices a ram, which is conveniently stuck in a nearby bush. As they begin their long journey home, we imagine Isaac slipping his hand into his father's hand and eyeing his father warily, as if perhaps a trust has been broken.

What just happened? Can love be reduced to a pass/fail test? How are we supposed to read this story?

View #1

Abraham passed the test because he was willing to sacrifice his son. While the story tells us that Abraham loves his son Isaac, it doesn't tell us if Abraham loves God. But even if he does, in this view, loving God isn't enough: Abraham needs to love God *more* than he loves Isaac. His willingness to sacrifice Isaac proves he loves God more than Isaac. The lesson from this view is that God needs us to give up what we love in order to prove we're worthy of keeping what we love.

We infer from this story that God will also test us to see if we really love God, and we'll only pass the test if we're one hundred percent willing to give up things that feel good (*masturbation, stretch denim,* People *magazine*) and be willing to do things that feel bad (*move to Africa, give up coffee, stay married to our abusive spouse*). If your partner asked you to take your dog—your only dog, the one you love—to the pound and put her down as a way to prove that you love your partner more than your dog, you'd probably start hatching a plan to put that relationship down instead. A loving partner shouldn't need to watch you put your dog down to prove your love. If you've spent any time believing in a God like that, you've probably felt like putting your relationship with that God down (*which seems like a perfectly reasonable thing to do*). There has to be more to see and more to know about love in this story.

View #2

Abraham was tested, but what is a test in the Bible? Is it pass/ fail? Is it open book? When do we have to put our pencils down? We can find clues to the answers in Deuteronomy 8:2, where the same word for test is used and also is defined: "God led the children of Israel through the wilderness to humble and test them in order to know what was in their hearts."

According to this definition, a test from God is designed to reveal what's already inside you—stuff you didn't even know was there. Even if what comes out isn't pretty, it is always a gift to see what's really true about yourself. A test like this helps you suspend reactive mind and get curious about why you do the things you do and whether you might be able to change. A test like this allows you to engage awareness in a new way, so you can return to Here.

> A test from God is designed to reveal what's already inside you—stuff you didn't even know was there. Even if what comes out isn't pretty, it is always a gift to see what's really true about yourself. ●

Starting about age four, I begged my dad to let me mow the

lawn. He finally relented when I was around eight, and I did a horrible job on my first try. Little tufts of grass were sticking up everywhere. But instead of fixing it himself, my dad took the time to show me how it looked, and he asked me to go back out there and fix it. This was a test, but it wasn't pass/fail. My dad showed me he believed I could do hard things and also that I could sometimes go back and fix my mistakes. That grass-cutting test was a gift that has served me my whole life.

View #3

To understand the story, we need to know about the prevailing cultural view of gods and humans and sacrifices during Abraham's life. Is Abraham's God like those other gods?

Based on what we know about his culture, Abraham's understanding of the gods was *transactional*. If you wanted a good crop or a son or a wife, you had to offer a sacrifice to whichever god managed the inventory for whatever you wanted. Given that, a story about a god demanding a meaningful sacrifice would have been par for the course. No one listening to the story at the time would have gasped as Abraham raised the knife to sacrifice his son; they would have expected the story to go that way. The gods are angry and need to be appeased. What would have made people gasp was how the story ends: with Isaac walking away alive.

Perhaps more than one test is going on in this story. What if the test was designed to draw out not only what's inside of

Abraham but also what's inside of God? Maybe the story starts the way it starts—with a god demanding a sacrifice—to pose a new question: Is the God of Abraham like all the other gods?

For the people originally listening to this story, the statement that Isaac walks away alive would invite them to engage a new awareness of a new kind of god. This God, the God of Abraham, wasn't transactional and didn't require child sacrifice. The God of Abraham seemed to see children as valuable and precious. The God of Abraham provided an unexpected sacrifice instead. The God of Abraham seemed to be motivated by something other than anger. The God of Abraham seemed to *love* Abraham. This was an entirely different kind of god, the kind that might cause people to abandon their views about what a god can be like.

Abandoning Our Views

The first view after reading this story seemed to reinforce the tired view of God that so many of us grew up with—one who requires us to sacrifice what we love and promise to do what we don't want to do. But in asking questions and searching for deeper layers of meaning, we saw that the story's original point might have been to help people discover a god who *wasn't* capricious, a god who *didn't* require them to sacrifice what they loved and promise to do what they didn't want to do. This story's original point might have been to introduce people to a god of love, rather than a *quid pro quo* god.

Whatever else the Bible is or isn't, it can't be a collection of stories designed to corroborate tired views of God that keep people stuck in reactive mind, convinced they'll only get the good stuff when they give up what they love. If the Bible is meant to help us return to Here in any real way, shouldn't its stories reveal the God who waits for us in this eternal Now with love? Shouldn't the Bible be willing to squirm as every generation poses new questions and waits for new answers?

I'm not suggesting that this homily on love and sacrifice was sufficient to rekindle your faith in the Bible, but I hope it invited you to see the Bible differently and perhaps abandon some of your views about it, rather than abandoning the Bible altogether. As you return to Here when reading the Bible, be mindful of when you are reading it with a reactive mind—hyper-aroused, looking for danger, convinced you're missing out on the good stuff—or with a receptive mind, willing to linger with your questions and even with the tension of not knowing, until you can see something new. ●

. . ● . .

Practice: Returning to Here by Letting the Bible Ask Us Questions

If we're going to ask the Bible our hard questions and watch it squirm before we accept its answers, I think it's fair to let it ask us a few open-ended questions that might make us squirm a little, too. Let's try out this practice on a Bible passage that includes Jesus.

In John 9, Jesus restores the sight of a man who was born blind, and then he immediately leaves town. When the religious leaders, the man's parents, and his neighbors in the village discover the guy can now see, they commence an elaborate investigation to try to get him to explain how it happened, but he never can, so no one's satisfied. As this long story gets longer and longer, everybody goes into reactive mind until finally the formerly blind guy is excommunicated from his village because he's now associated with a dangerous heretic (*who no one can find and about whom no one really knows anything*). It's a classic scapegoat story—so familiar we can't even see when we perpetuate that kind of response ourselves.

This story is intriguing for many reasons, but perhaps the most beguiling is that Jesus spends exactly zero time explaining himself to those religious leaders, parents, and neighbors. The man doesn't even see Jesus again until the very end of the story, when he runs into Jesus outside of the community. Finally, Jesus breaks his silence and explains, in an uncharacteristically open way, exactly who he is. Jesus remains enigmatic to anyone who demands an explanation for how or why he spends so much time restoring that which ordinary people have lost. But he remains accessible and unambiguously helpful to anyone who cries out to be touched, to be welcomed, and to have their humanity restored to them after it has been taken away.

It's easy to get stuck in reactive mind when reading this story. Maybe you get stuck trying to figure out whether the healing is literal or metaphorical. Maybe you get stuck trying to use this story as proof that the awful people who scapegoated you are evil, blind losers whom Jesus would automatically reject. Maybe you get stuck because you can't see anything surprising or new at all. But what if you linger with the story long enough to try to see yourself in each of the characters? What new places might you discover to which you can return and find the God who is eternally waiting for you with love?

Can you see yourself in the blind person? In what ways have your genuine experiences with God been misunderstood by people who couldn't get over a view of God that still requires a sacrifice? If you've been scapegoated, how might you find hope in seeing a God who is Christlike, who wants to heal you anyway?

Can you see yourself in the religious leaders, parents, and villagers? If you realize you've scapegoated someone rather than taking the time to try to understand their experience of God, what invitation might there be for you? Try to notice without judging yourself. What new view(s) of God might you be willing to consider?

Can you see yourself in Jesus? Maybe you'll notice how you're tempted to defend something you've done, or a belief you have, with people who aren't ready to hear it or to see you. Maybe you'll sense an invitation to stop trying to defend yourself to them. Maybe you'll even feel permission to leave town and spend your time with those who are willing to receive what you have to give.

Reading the Bible with a receptive mind might turn out to be one of the most redemptive things you've ever done. But even then, reading the Bible will probably remain tricky. There are so many genres, so many generational differences, so much mystery, and just so much going on that we'll never find a way to be completely satisfied by the Bible. And I think it's perfectly reasonable to put the Bible down for long seasons if you feel too triggered by it. But take heart. As Meister Eckhart might remind us, if our search for God is limited even to the way of the Bible, we might end up with the Bible but miss out on God. ●

· · ● · ·

Practice: Returning to Here by Practicing Silence

While rekindling our faith sometimes looks like changing how we respond to email or how we read the Bible, it also can look like a return to Here when we aren't doing anything at all. That feels a lot like befriending Here in silence or our own solitude.

There's no wrong way to enter into silence, unless of course you bring anything with you, which of course you will, so I guess there is a wrong way into silence after all. Like all good contemplative practices, there is a loophole, if you're still interested: as long as you're okay with getting it wrong, you can go right ahead and enter into silence as free as a bird. (*Incidentally, that's the option I'd recommend, with one caveat: you'll still hate getting it wrong.*)

Here's how you might start. Pick a consistent place where you'll be free from interruptions and pick a consistent time when you'll do it each day. If you're a morning person, do it then, but if you're a night owl, do it then. It doesn't matter when you do it; it just matters that you set an intention to sit in silence for a period of time and actually do it. If you're new to this, I'd suggest trying to sit in silence for five minutes at first.

You might want to sit in a comfortable chair or on a mat on the floor, or you might want to lie down; it doesn't matter, as long as you're comfortable. You might want to light a candle or sit in the dark. Start by taking a deep breath in, let it out, set a timer for five minutes, and close your eyes.

When you sit in silence, you're not trying to find God or hear from God or think any profound thoughts. Don't even try to return to Here. Just follow your breath in and out, breathing normally. And before you're even aware of it, your reactive mind will start chattering. When you become aware that it's talking to you, don't judge yourself or those thoughts. Just smile, welcome those thoughts by briefly saying hello, then picture them floating by, like clouds in the sky or a leaf in a river, and return to your breath. At some point, your reactive mind will convince you that you forgot to set a timer; five minutes is a long time when you're attending to your breath and trying to be polite to your distracting thoughts—the longest five minutes of your life. Hello, reactive mind. Smile. Then watch that thought as it floats away.

You may wonder what practicing silence does (*other than drive you crazy*), but if you really need to know, it's a training process for your reactive mind to realize it doesn't always have to be on duty. It's like training a puppy. At first, that puppy's one job will be to nip at you with those razor-sharp baby teeth, destroying your clothes and your couch cushions, but over time, she'll grow her permanent teeth and settle down. After enough sessions of sitting in silence for five minutes a day, your reactive mind will settle down during the rest of your day, too, not just when you sit in silence. More and more, especially when you're anxious and overstimulated, you'll be able to return to Here, where God is always waiting for you with love, in the eternal Now. ⬡

● ● ● ● ●

Practice: Returning to Here through Contemplative Prayer

Like practicing silence, contemplative prayer involves detaching from the hyper-aroused reactive mind and learning to rest in God with what is. In contemplative prayer, we're present to the goodness of God in this moment, depending on God to give us what we need in order to love, grow, and become ourselves. Thomas Merton was committed to a life of contemplative prayer, but for him, it was not a way to find God. Rather, it was a way to rest in the God who has already found us. It turned him away from the overstimulation of the world toward God. He found that it was a way to get where he needed to go by learning to be where he was. Merton didn't see contemplative prayer as a way to escape from the world, though. It was a way to more fully engage in the world, as dark as it actually is, without being consumed by the darkness.

There are countless forms of contemplative prayer. A simple form is centering prayer, which is similar to practicing silence but with the addition of a focus word, phrase, or sacred object. You could start with ten minutes, slowly moving up to twenty or even thirty minutes when you get comfortable with it. The following suggestions for entering into contemplative prayer are adapted from Father Thomas Keating's four movements to centering prayer:

1. Sitting comfortably, choose a sacred word (for example, love, God, or Jesus) as the symbol of your intention to consent to God's presence and action within.

2. Some people gaze at an object (a cross or a lit candle) in order to help focus their attention, while others prefer closing their eyes. Either way, when you are ready, bring the sacred word to your mind, symbolizing your consent to God's presence and action within.

3. When you become aware of any stray thoughts or worries, accept their presence without judgment, then watch them float away as you gently return to your sacred word.

4. At the end of the prayer period, remain in silence with eyes closed for a couple of minutes.

Practicing attentiveness is learning to gently return to Here whenever you notice that your reactive mind has convinced you to run away from Now or to pine for something you're missing. Practicing attentiveness allows you to listen to a different voice, the one calling you to become who you are. ●

We Must Abandon God

One person said they had God,
while another lamented God's absence.

I say this: we must abandon the God
we have in our thinking and believing

for God's sake, so that we might come
to know God as God truly is—who

never left us, beyond knowing, in
a single oneness and pure union.

PRACTICE

Ordinariness

To become aware and awake to who I am, I
practice ordinariness: learning to return to who I
am and away from who I think I should be.

I want to be happy. I also want to be successful and necessary. I want a job that provides personal meaning and also
financial security. I want relationships where I am loved and
also admired. I want to be decisive, and I also want to be
right. On my journey to attain those things, I will learn to
hide who I am and to play the role of who I should be, carefully following a script whose plot is written for me to get
what I want. I will end up lost and isolated, far away from
home. Perhaps returning to who I am starts with choosing
which *me* I'm talking about.

● ● ◆ ● ●

Wait a Minute, Which Me Am I Supposed to Be?

Recently, worrying that an upcoming conversation would go badly, I emailed my two sisters and my parents for encouragement. They cheered me on, piling on generous dollops of praise for my ability to think on my feet and do well in these types of conversations. They told me to just be myself, and everything would take care of itself.

But then I panicked a little. Which version of myself should I be? The one that rambles on and on until I finally say what I think they need to hear? Or the one that carefully shaves the edges off in order to avoid conflict? Or the one that has nothing to lose? Or the one that has everything to lose? Or the one that is trying to believe he has nothing to lose but fears he has everything to lose? Or the one that overanalyzes everything? And what version of myself will show up that day? Sometimes I'm insecure, and other times I have a quiet and effortless confidence. Some days I'm willing to be vulnerable, and other days even the smallest criticism is a knockout punch. And anyway, constantly wondering how well I did at being who I am is not being who I am. Carefully mapping out a strategy to be who I am is not being who I am. No wonder I panicked. It's like I'm trying to follow a script nobody else has even seen.

I'm currently obsessed with a dark comedy on HBO called *Barry*. Bill Hader plays an assassin named Barry Berkman, who believes he's only good at killing people. In the pilot, he follows one of his marks into an acting class populated exclusively by extraordinarily shitty but sincere acting students. As Barry sits in the back of a small, dark theater, he watches Gene Cousineau (*brilliantly played by Henry Winkler*), a washed-out actor turned teacher, coax those students to commit to fully bringing themselves to their roles. As the class ends, Barry's wonderstruck eyes say it all: he's home. Barry waits in the dark parking lot and watches Cousineau climb into his oversized SUV (*which perfectly matches his oversized ego*) and start driving away. But Barry can't help himself; he approaches the car and taps on the window. Before Cousineau can even get his window all the way down, Barry blurts out his story:

> You want to know what I'm good at? I'm good at killing people. You know, when I got back from Afghanistan, I was really depressed. You know, like, I didn't leave my house for months. And this friend of my dad's, he's—he's like an uncle to me—he helped me out, and he gave me a purpose. He told me that what I was good at over there could be useful here. And it's a job. You know? The money's good. And

these people I take out, like, they're bad people. But lately, you know, I've—like, I'm not sleeping, and—that depressed feeling's back, you know? Like—like, I know there's more to me than that. But maybe—I don't know—maybe it's not. Maybe this is all I'm good at. Anyway, forget it. Sorry to bother you.

Cousineau misunderstands Barry's startling confession, assuming it's a monologue he has prepared in order to enroll in the class. "Where's that from?" he asks.

Again, Barry's eyes say everything. "What?" he asks.

Cousineau's eyes narrow. "Are you telling me that was an improvisation? Interesting. The story's nonsense, but there's something to work with. My class is not cheap."

In between assassinating people, Barry attends Cousineau's class, and he's terrible. Because he refuses to tell his story, he's unable to access any real emotion as he rehearses scenes. Cousineau's pithy acting mantras—*Use it! Make the unsafe choice! Commit to you!*—make it harder and harder for Barry to hide who he is. He desperately wants to come clean to his new acting friends but keeps getting entangled with his old script as an assassin. The writers of the show create a beautiful paradox: it's only by committing fully to acting that Barry has any hope of returning to himself.

Cousineau's acting class became an unexpected opportunity for Barry to choose to practice ordinariness and return to himself. Practicing ordinariness is learning to see and embrace the unexpected opportunities in our own lives that can help us return to ourselves. Practicing ordinariness is learning to recognize the real you buried underneath all the bad dialogue you've memorized and choosing the real you instead of continuing to follow a script. The real you doesn't need to follow a script; the real you knows how to improvise.

Here's the thing with just being ourselves: over the course of our lives, based on the unique cocktail of our families of origin, our personalities, our failures, successes, wounds and many other factors, we have curated quite a few "false selves" so we can pick the one that has the best chance of getting what we want and need in many different situations. Without our even being conscious of it, each of those false selves is following a script designed to get what it thinks it needs.

For those aware enough to want to return to their ordinariness—their true selves—it's helpful to become aware of the triggers, or scripts, that keep us from being who we really are. God is eternally waiting for us with love, but because our false selves are illusory, they'd simply vanish if they showed up to meet with God. Because we can only meet God with our true selves, we need to learn to identify the scripts we're following that keep us trapped in our false selves and unable to meet with God. A great place to start is by learning to get curious about those uncomfortable moments where we get triggered.

• • ● • •

Practice: Becoming Aware of Triggers That Keep You on Script

Years ago, I sat in a therapist's office, trying to recover from a devastating relational loss. When I first saw the therapist, he warned me that he was almost always late for appointments and that he swore like a sailor. "If either of those things is going to bother you," he told me, "this probably isn't going to work."

I was struck by how he owned who he was; he didn't even pretend to be "working on" those two things (*by the way, I loved that he swore like a sailor and I got used to him being late, which he always was*). I'm sure he said the same thing to all his patients, but it didn't sound like a script, it sounded like he knew who he was.

Months into our sessions together, I told him that my greatest fear was that this devastating relational loss was all my fault. He looked at me and immediately said, "Oh, I'm positive it's all your fault." My brain quickly kicked into reactive mind; I got triggered big time. The character in my script always finds a way to avoid being at fault. I considered peppering the conversation with some foul language of my own, but I eventually settled on simply furrowing my brow. "Now that we've settled that," he said with a smile, "you can

44

walk all the way down that plank, jump off, and learn how to be Steve Wiens for the rest of your life."

I might have preferred it if he had tried to convince me it wasn't my fault, but that would have prevented me from seeing the script I was following. I was stuck playing a character who needed to be wildly successful at everything he did—and I mean everything. I was in this therapist's office because I was trying not to get booed off the stage. I was stuck in reactive mind; my only options were complete success or utter failure.

When my therapist told me he was positive the loss of that relationship was all my fault, he was trying to make me break character. It worked. For the first time in my life, I saw how hard I had worked at trying to be wildly successful. I also saw I couldn't pull off that role because I care too much about whether people like me; people who are always wildly successful are usually assholes. He helped me see that I could jump off the complete success/utter failure plank, as long as I was willing to flail around in midair for a while, learning how to be Steve Wiens for the rest of my life. That sounded scary but freeing. I considered getting curious about starting to tell people what my own "two things" were so I could find a way to stop furrowing my brow so often: "Hi! I will probably present several fake versions of myself to you until I feel safe, and I need plenty of verbal affirmation if this relationship is going to work, so—"

Building on what I learned in therapy, I've come to see that the reactive mind tries to stay in control and keep everything predictable, which is the opposite of a life of faith. But rekindling a faith that is honest starts with being willing to give up control and predictability (*your scripts*), as scary as that sounds.

What are your triggers? What keeps you stuck in reactive mind and following your script? What keeps you from returning to ordinariness, to your true self?

> What are your triggers? What keeps you stuck in reactive mind and following your script? What keeps you from returning to ordinariness, to your true self? ●

Maybe you're triggered when you feel like life is slipping out of control, despite your best efforts at planning for a life that will stay in control. Maybe you're triggered when you lose something that felt essential to your security and survival—for instance, when you get laid off from a job or a relationship ends. Maybe you're triggered when you feel as if someone doesn't approve of you or a project you worked really hard at, despite how hard you tried to get the other person to like you and it.

Here's the thing: when we write our scripts, we also write lines we expect God (*and everybody else*) to follow too, so our story can keep unfolding the way we've written it. When our life starts slipping out of control, or we've lost something that felt essential to our well-being, or we can't seem to get the approval we worked so hard to get, we blame God. This is understandable because the God you wrote in your script didn't come through. When we get triggered, we're tempted to plunge into reactive mind, which demands we grab onto whatever trapeze is in front of us instead of seeing what new opportunities might reveal themselves if we can linger in midair for just a little longer. If we can linger in that moment, our triggers can actually set us free from our scripts and allow us to return to ordinariness.

Father Thomas Keating understood the architecture of our scripts, or false selves, as our "program for happiness." He explained that for children to come to know who they are and differentiate themselves from others, they need appropriate levels of three things: (1) power and control; (2) security and survival; and (3) affection and esteem. To the degree that a child does not get those basic needs met, the child will learn to overidentify with one of them, writing a script to ensure they get what they need. When we were younger, we needed our programs for happiness in order to survive, and we can be grateful to them for helping us get to where we are now.

But, here's the thing: our programs for happiness work until they don't. The way we can tell they aren't working anymore is that we realize that God—and life itself—isn't following our script anymore (*and never did to begin with*), and our triggers get stronger and stronger until it hurts so bad we decide we have to change. The good news (*which might feel like bad news at first*) is that the god you wrote in your script is illusory, too, like your false self. When you return to ordinariness and abandon your script, that illusory god vanishes, too, which can leave you feeling off balance for a little while.

> But, here's the thing: our programs for happiness work until they don't. The way we can tell they aren't working anymore is that we realize that God—and life itself—isn't following our script anymore (and never did to begin with) . . . ●

As you learn to return to ordinariness and find God waiting for you with love in the eternal Now, two practices will help you stay aware and awake to yourself. The first is to notice without judging, and the second is to tell the truth as it really is. ●

· · ◆ · ·

Practice: Noticing without Judging

What script are you following? What is the most important thing for your character to achieve or maintain? If you can simply notice when you are following a script and refrain from judging yourself for doing so, you're already breaking character; you're already halfway down the plank. Noticing without judging means you observe yourself playing your character, but without needing to shame yourself or feel frustrated that you keep doing it. You probably wouldn't shame a friend for falling back into their script (*unless they had just given up coffee or nicotine*). You'd probably say something like "It's okay. You're doing the best you can. Just keep walking down that plank."

If your script involves maintaining power and control, you probably spend a lot of energy keeping secrets. Your character might try to exert power over people through positional authority or through passive-aggressive posturing. Your false self might need to control your environment through excessive list making, helping others until you resent them, or constantly trying to fix things and people. When you notice yourself doing any of those things, breathe, close your eyes, and say to yourself, "It's okay. You're doing the best you can. My ordinary self doesn't have to be perfect. God is with me as I am."

If your script involves maintaining security and survival, you probably worry a lot about the future. If your character needs money to feel secure, your false self will work extraordinarily hard to make as much money as it can. Your false self may spend a lot of energy making sure nobody gets too close, creating elaborate boundaries to keep people out. If you assume being in a relationship will make you feel safe and secure, you'll do whatever it takes to find one and stay in it. When you notice yourself doing any of those things, breathe, close your eyes, and say to yourself, "It's okay. You're doing the best you can. My ordinary self isn't on its own. God is with me as I am."

If your script involves maintaining affection and esteem, you spend a lot of energy hustling for approval. You've become an expert at trying to sense exactly what you need to do so you can get the affection you so badly want. Even when someone who genuinely loves you asks you what you need or how you feel, you can't access your own truth. When you notice yourself doing any of those things, you might breathe, close your eyes, and say to yourself, "It's okay. You're doing the best you can. My ordinary self is in there, and God will help me locate him/her/them."

Becoming aware and awake to who you really are requires naming how much energy you've spent following a script based on playing the role of a character you thought you should be. If you are going to jump off the plank of that script, you have to know why you chose that script and why you kept trying to play the role of that character. Practicing ordinariness is returning to who you are. It's the process of learning to be "you" for the rest of your life. ⬢

· ● ● ● ·

Practice: Telling the Truth as It Really Is

Learning to improvise when you've spent a lifetime following a script is hard, but it's possible. There are no guarantees about what will happen when you decide to tell the truth, but the risk is worth it because no matter how anybody else responds, telling the truth as it really is cultivates ordinariness. When you find yourself in a safe place where you are invited to tell the truth as it really is, take the risk and tell the truth.

Consider how this plays out in the HBO series *Barry*. In the middle of the second season, Barry finds himself at Cousineau's apartment, shattered because he almost killed a guy who wasn't one of his marks; he was just really angry. He can't hide any longer. Cousineau drops the mantras and becomes a mentor. Barry is covering his eyes in shame, but Cousineau doesn't hold back. He tenderly invites Barry to tell the truth: "You want to tell this story. You need to tell this story."

Barry somehow finds the courage to meet Cousineau's eyes. "You'll look at me differently," he croaks.

"I promise you I will not look at you differently," Cousineau says. "Now. What happened?"

After Barry reveals the secret of what really happened in Afghanistan, Cousineau reveals his own secret: he was a terrible father to his son, and he regrets it deeply, but he believes people can change. "How?" Barry asks.

In that moment, Cousineau becomes the father he wished he would have been. "Barry, we're doing it right now. We're talking about your feelings instead of acting out your feelings."

Then Barry pauses and asks the question that has been haunting him the entire show: "Do you think I'm a terrible person?"

Cousineau doesn't hesitate, and his answer comes from a deep place of truth. "I think you are deeply human. You did a terrible thing. But do I think that defines you? No."

When Barry opens up to Cousineau, we can see that he is afraid, but we also see he's willing to let go of the trapeze of his false self, so he at least has a chance of grabbing onto his true self. When you find yourself in similar situations, and you choose to hang in midair, you'll probably be afraid, too, like you're plunging to your death. Or it might feel liberating, like you're finally floating free. Lingering in that place (*hamakom*) will get you where you need to go. Practicing ordinariness is essentially the celebration of being deeply human. It's about helping someone else celebrate their deep humanity, despite the terrible things they've done.

Eventually, you have to go off script if you want to shine like the sun. ◆

Within Me in That Soft Place

Within me in the soft place
we call the soul is a fortress

so strong and beyond all
knowing that no one can

enter, not I, not those I
love or fear, not even You.

In this citadel, I am truly
Who I am beyond how I

know myself and how
others know me and there

You are truly You beyond
the names we have chosen

To give you, and here we
are not united but one.

Simplicity

To touch life deeply in every moment, I practice simplicity: giving unambiguous yeses and unapologetic noes in ways that leave margin and space.

The internet has made it possible for someone in Fayetteville, Arkansas, and someone in Monument, Colorado, to "talk" using only their thumbs. Back in the day, if you wanted to get in touch with someone across state lines, you had to write a letter or, if you could afford long-distance rates, call them. Those were your options—unless, of course, you were an especially creative seventh-grade kid who lived 5,592 miles away from his best friends.

In 1983, when I was entering seventh grade, my family moved from Oxnard, California, to Waterloo, Belgium, and I missed my friends. Because my monthly allowance only covered the occasional can of Coke, Snickers bar, or ticket to the movies, an overseas long-distance phone call was out of the question. I can distinctly remember envisioning how totally rad a "video phone" would be, though I was pretty sure flying cars would come first. Lacking such a device, I popped a ninety-minute cassette tape into my boom box, and on both sides of the tape, I recorded myself telling stories and thoughts about my daily life in Belgium: *They sell beer at McDonald's! I don't think people wear deodorant here! There's a weird little toilet next to the regular toilet that sprays water in your butt, and I'm afraid to use it!* When the tape was full, I mailed it to one of my friends, though it took at least two weeks to get there. My friend got another blank tape and recorded stories and thoughts about his daily life back in Oxnard: *Went to the beach today! Do you think Han Solo will get out of that frozen carbonite? Do you think Vanna White is kind of hot?* Every month or so, as long as my friend remembered to do it *(he usually did),* I'd get a new tape. We didn't have internet, but we did have ingenuity. Those tapes would be priceless to me today if we had saved them; of course, we didn't—we were seventh-grade boys.

It's now 2019, and flying cars still don't exist, but I do have a battery-powered global broadcast system that fits in my pocket and gives me limitless "video phone" capabilities anywhere in the world. It also lets me stream limitless movies and television shows late into the night, and it enables my twelve-year-old son to send me texts when I'm at work. It lets me listen to podcasts on limitless subjects, ranging from the history of gnomes to celebrities interviewing other celebrities about celebrity. It also lets me publicly share my limitless reactions to, well, everything.

Jesus, take the wheel, as my friend Rebecca would say.

What I'm trying to say is that everything feels too limitless. There are too many choices of what to watch on Netflix, too many opinions from too many people on too many current events, and honestly, too many topics to care deeply about. I can't process it all. I don't want to live off the grid, but I do want to be able to reclaim where my grid ends and where everybody else's grid begins. I need to touch my edges.

> I don't want to live off the grid, but I do want to be able to reclaim where my grid ends and where everybody else's grid begins. I need to touch my edges. ●

Like the rest of us, Jesus got tired and cranky, but he seemed to have a clear sense of where he ended and where everybody else began. He seemed to know his own limits, and even with all the love and care he poured out, he seemed to prioritize getting what he needed.

One night, after a long day surrounded by people and their needs, Jesus climbed into a boat and then miraculously calmed a storm. When I try to imagine this story, I see Jesus stumbling slowly behind the disciples as they walk toward the boat, utterly exhausted from a long day with too many people and too many needs. Jesus is so tired they have to stand alongside him so he doesn't fall in the water as he climbs into the boat. Once onboard, he goes below and collapses on the nearest seat cushion, falling asleep within seconds. Suddenly, the disciples are shaking him awake. Mercilessly battered by wind, the boat is beginning to splinter apart as a nasty storm rages. Instead of wrapping him in a life preserver, they scream at him, "Do something! Don't you care that we're about to die?" When he realizes how severe the problem is, Jesus talks to the wind and the waves. "Peace," he says. "Be still." The boat continues to rock back and forth for a minute or two, and the sails are in tatters, but the lake has become an unbroken expanse of utter calm. Jesus interrupts the unexpected tranquility with a question that may be over the top, but everybody's cranky when they first wake up: "Why were you guys so afraid? Do you still have no faith?" Then he goes back to sleep. Before assessing the damage to the boat, two of the disciples light cigarettes and wonder out loud just who in the hell this guy is.

Even if you doubt how someone who is neither part of the X-Men nor one of the Avengers can change the weather, you have to admire a guy who can sleep through a storm. Why was he able to tune out the storm when everyone else was so terrorized by it? Why was he able to get the rest he needed when the heavens themselves seemed to be conspiring to keep him awake?

Practicing simplicity is like being able to sleep through a storm: you're able to get what you need, live within your limits, and make time for what's really important in the middle of the storm of overstimulation, busyness, and overcommitment that's sweeping everybody else overboard. Practicing simplicity doesn't mean you have to forgo digital music or buy a five-pack of blank cassette tapes. It doesn't mean you have to delete your Facebook account after an all-night binge of scrolling while finishing off that pan of brownies one forkful at a time. It doesn't mean getting nostalgic about those trips to Family Video. What it does involve is learning to touch life deeply in every moment by learning to give unambiguous yeses and unapologetic noes in ways that leave margin and space.

> . . . is learning to touch life deeply in every moment by learning to give unambiguous yeses and unapologetic nos in ways that leave margin and space. ●

Maybe that sounds like a fairy-tale life. Maybe you feel trapped by a thousand things demanding your yes. Maybe *no* is a four-letter word in your particular family, workplace, or group of friends. Maybe margin and space feel like luxuries you can't afford. Maybe you're afraid the storm will keep you awake no matter how hard you try to get some sleep.

Don't focus on the storm. Go down below, where it's quiet. Beyond the thousand demands of your life lies a question, which you will hear when it gets quiet enough. But when you finally hear it, don't answer too quickly. Here it is: *What are you willing to say no to, so you can create space to say yes to what you really want?*

· · ● · ·

Practice: Writing a Simplicity Sentence

One of the ways to discover what you really want is to write a phrase that describes what you're most dedicated to—a statement that is big enough to hold deep meaning but focused enough to be a filter for ordering your life and your relationships. If you were limited to thirty words or less, how would you describe the people and activities that are most important to you? One person might write, "Inventing things that delight people and experiencing one-of-a-kind adventures by myself and with the people I love"—that's twenty words. Someone else might say they're dedicated to "assisting others in the transformation of pain and the restoration of hope"— that's only thirteen words!

If God is eternally waiting for you with love in a moment called Now, you'll find surprising nourishment by becoming present to God before, during, and after you attempt to write your phrase. But try to resist the temptation to see God as looking over your shoulder, making sure you say the right thing. Writing your phrase isn't trying to hit a bull's-eye. Trust that a loving presence will guide you where you need to go. Writing your simplicity phrase is the kind of test we saw with Abraham; it's designed to bring the good stuff out of you that you didn't even know was in there. It isn't a pass/fail test, and you only have to put your pencil down when you're good and ready.

If you need help writing your phrase, try this: at the end of each day, spend ten minutes recording the activities you chose to do that day with your free time (*no need to record everyday activities like meals or working*). You might be tempted to cheat and not write down the two hours you spent on Amazon, so try to just record what you actually did without judging yourself. End each day by rating your level of satisfaction with the choices you made (*1 = totally unsatisfied; 10 = perfect day*). For example: *Got up a half an hour early to meditate; Ate lunch at my desk to catch up on email; Called a friend on the way home from work; Folded laundry; Watched two hours of Netflix after dinner; skipped my workout; went to bed at 11pm. Six hours of sleep last night. Satisfaction level: 6.* At the end of your week, look at your daily choices and see if your choices line up with your simplicity phrase. What are you doing that you want to stop doing, or do less? What aren't you doing that you want to start doing? This exercise can help you choose to spend your time doing more of what's really important to you.

This practice can help you set priorities, but the storm of a margin-less life will still sweep you overboard unless you enforce those priorities. This involves learning to respond to demands on your time with clear yeses and unapologetic no's that correspond to your simplicity phrase. ●

●　●　●　●　●

Practice: Saying No to Wasted Time

When you've named what you want, it's time to start saying no to everything that keeps you from living that kind of life. If Jesus could take a nap in the middle of a storm when everybody else was freaking out, you can say no to playing Words with Friends at midnight.

How much time and energy do we spend doing—or considering doing—tasks that take us beyond our limits and away from what we love most? Why do we do this? A few months ago, my friend Nick noticed he was too tethered to his smartphone, but he couldn't get rid of it altogether because he needed it for work.

Most of us would say we probably use our phone too much, but Nick is way more intentional than most of us. He's serious about saying no to time wasters so he can say yes to what he really wants to do. Nick set up his phone plan to charge him by the minute and by the text message. With that financial incentive, he uses the device only when he needs it. One of the hardest parts, he told me, has been relearning how to find an address without GPS. But as long as he plans a little extra time to get lost, and as long as he's willing to stop and ask for directions, he enjoys trying to navigate without GPS. In addition to having more time to do what he loves, making this change has helped him be even more creative.

With the time he freed up, Nick has invented a printing press, a string of programmable blinking lights for a costume his daughter wore for Halloween, and a machine that makes perfectly clear blocks of ice for the delicious cocktails he prepares for guests. He knows what he wants, and he creates space to do it. If you're thinking, "Must be nice," consider that Nick is able to do what he wants because he says no to wasting time. "People are always asking me how I have time to invent stuff or to go on the adventures we go on, and it's not like I live a life of leisure," he told me. "I work full time, and I participate in what it takes to keep our house clean and running and all that stuff, but I guess I don't waste a lot of time doing things that aren't important to me. What are they doing with their time, I want to ask them."

"It's like my mind is working the way it did before internet," Nick told me, his eyes shining with quiet confidence.

Nick's really smart, but I don't think he's any more capable than you or me. This is simplicity: he sleeps just fine on the bottom of the boat while most of the rest of us are getting swept overboard by a storm of wasted time and energy.

Saying the confident *no* can open up space for quiet and energy for survival. One of my friends blocks off the entire month of January to "bunk in." She's an introvert, so for that month, she says no to leaving her house for reasons other than work and what's absolutely necessary to make life function. This disappoints some people, but she knows she needs to create space for herself. In other situations, saying no becomes an urgent need when an unexpected storm blows in: a cancer diagnosis, the loss of a loved one, or an accident, for example. When these events knock you overboard and leave you afraid you're going to drown, practicing simplicity can be a matter of sheer survival. When you emerge from your grief, practicing simplicity can help you discover a larger purpose for your life.

Saying no is especially powerful when combined with a yes to something better. A couple of years ago, my seventy-three-year-old dad got really serious about getting back in shape. He said no to some bad habits and yes to exercise and eating well. His increased energy and significant weight loss created space for him to say yes to many new things. Similarly, two friends recently decided to say no to trying to do life without help and yes to medication for depression and anxiety. It's hard (*especially for men*) to admit there's something wrong with our brain chemistry that makes every day foggy and overcast, but because of their no (*and their yes*), they're experiencing a greater capacity to pursue what they really want in life.

What gets your unapologetic no? ●

● ● ● ● ●

Practice: Saying Yes to a Larger Purpose

Paula D'Arcy was twenty-seven years old when a drunk driver killed her husband and twenty-one-month-old daughter. Paula was three months pregnant and in the car during the accident but survived unharmed. Suddenly, Paula found herself trying to grieve the death of her husband and daughter, including the loss of the future she'd expected to have with them, while also preparing for the brand-new baby girl growing inside her.

"Everything that pretends to be a matter of life and death but isn't, revealed itself," she later discovered. The questions she asked in her grief—"Is there a God bigger than this tragedy? What is the meaning of life?"—weren't heady and intellectual; they were matters of life and death. She wasn't going to make it unless she found real answers. Those questions led her to begin praying what she would later call the first honest prayer of her life: "God, if you are really out there and if you are real, then help me, let me find you, show me who you are."

She soon found herself meeting with Dr. Norman Vincent Peale, the renowned psychologist. After telling him the entire story of her loss, within which she was still so lost, he gave her an invitation that profoundly changed her life. "Young woman," he said, "you've got a huge challenge in front of you: to discover the purpose of your life."

Paula replied honestly and quickly. "I lost the purpose of my life when my husband and daughter died." Dr. Peale held her gaze with steady kindness and grounded wisdom and said, "You lost the purpose you wanted. But your life has a larger purpose, because you are still alive. And the thing that you're searching so hard for, you already have."

Paula's grief eventually led her to experience a major shift: from a God *out there* to a God *within*. Paula later discovered what she really wanted to say yes to: helping others find meaning in the midst of profound loss. After nearly twenty years of leading workshops and seminars to help people transform their pain and unresolved grief, she founded The Red Bird Foundation, a nonprofit designed to provide the means to touch the hearts and lives of those who have experienced profound loss but have limited resources and little hope, as well as to train those who want to participate in bringing about that change. Paula D'Arcy says that the

defining, unchanging dedication of the Red Bird Foundation is to "to assist in the movement of love in this world
and at this time." I find the simplicity of that dedication to
be incredibly moving. It's big enough to hold deep meaning
but focused enough to act as a filter for what they will do and
what they won't do.

As Paula's story shows us, simplicity *is* about getting
what you need, but it isn't *just* about getting what you need.
The story of Jesus calming the storm makes the same point.

Immediately after Jesus calmed the storm, the disciples
steered the boat to the eastern shore of the Sea of Galilee
and docked in a region called the Garasenes, which roughly
means "a stranger drawing near." Immediately after getting
out of the boat, a stranger "with an impure spirit" came
"from the tombs" to meet Jesus (Mark 5:2). Apparently, this
guy lived among the dead and was so dangerous that when
people tried to chain him up, he snapped those chains as if
they were Silly String. No one could subdue him, so the story
goes. Every night, as people tried to go to sleep, they heard
the man howling as he cut himself to ribbons with rocks. So
if a storm scared the disciples to death, I can't imagine how
they reacted to this guy.

When the man saw Jesus from a distance, he ran to him,
fell to his knees, and begged Jesus not to torture him. Jesus
wasn't terrified by the stranger who drew near. After identify-
ing that the man was demon possessed, Jesus cast the impure

spirits out of the man and sent them into a herd of pigs, which promptly ran off a cliff and drowned in the lake. Afterward, the shocked townspeople found the man "dressed and in his right mind" (5:15) and chatting with Jesus. Because Jesus knew how to sleep in a storm, he also knew how to help a stranger wake up to his own humanity.

> Because Jesus knew how to sleep in a storm, he also knew how to help a stranger wake up to his own humanity. ●

When you become a person with margins who stays responsive to what's important, you will carry an inner authority that will be irresistible to strangers who need a safe place to rediscover their humanity. Your presence will calm many storms. Simplicity isn't only about helping others get what they need; it can be about helping them say yes to their own life. ●

· ● ◆ ● ·

Your Single Yes of Love

Often the little things annoy me
    and the big ones seem to gallop
with their shades of gloom
    and shake off even the radiant

sun-splashed light of today,
    and I know I should hoe the
virtue of patience but do not,
    and all my hurry unravels

my careful plans for calm
    and worries away thoughts
of long-off better times.
    And then I hear You say again

that you are without why
    and ask that I let go of
all this in the simple joy
    of Your single Yes of Love.

Rhythm

To live in harmony with those around me, I
practice rhythm: learning to hear and play my
part in the song the universe is singing.

My friend Will and I share a love for good bourbon, early-1970s Ford Broncos, late-night conversations, and more recently, jazz. Will is a gifted jazz musician; he plays the clarinet, the saxophone, and the bass guitar. What hooked me on jazz was Will explaining to me that the essence of jazz is story.

The story of jazz began in New Orleans in the early twentieth century, when African rhythm, blues, and improvisation fused with European harmony and instrumentation. Jazz is made up of two complementary but seemingly opposite energies: rhythm and improvisation. Each musician needs to know the blueprint of each song, the set of predetermined chords that accompany the basic melody. But on each successive chorus, the different instruments take turns improvising solos. Each time the song is played, it becomes something familiar but brand new.

"What jazz brings is emotion," Will explained. "As each player improvises their solo, they bring where they came from, what happened the night before, and what is going on in their lives at that moment. All of those factors are reflected in their short time of improvisation. Their instruments become an extension of their voice."

Pausing to take a slow puff from his cigar, Will smiled as he blew a plume of white smoke over his left shoulder. He looked down at his feet and then right into my eyes. "No other music exposes so much of a person's soul, so much of their story."

When a group of musicians are held together by a shared rhythm, they are free to express their unique story through their improvised solos in time with the rhythm. Those solos may be different each time they play the song, depending on what is happening in their lives in that unique moment in time. But it's the shared rhythm that brings the song together each time it's played, even when the solos morph and change. When a jazz musician struggles to hear the rhythm or can't find the notes, the other musicians are able to help them remember the song by playing back what they have heard.

Like good jazz, the universe also has a rhythm, a deep bass line that keeps all of creation in time. And deep within each human being is a unique song, reflecting that person's truest nature and purpose in life. You were born with your song; the divine breath gave it to you. But as you received and perpetuated pain, loss, and shame, you lost the ability to hear it. You need to find a way to remember it, but you probably can't remember it alone.

· ● ·

Your Story Is Your Song

When we forget our song, we become tired, lonely, and disconnected—from God, from our own souls, and from the rest of creation.

In *What Is My Song?*, their retelling of a traditional African fable, Dennis, Sheila, and Matthew Linn tell the story of Deo, an East African child whose mother sang his song to him over and over again while he was growing in her belly. Deo was born knowing his song. One day, though, Deo commits an act of violence against his friend Matani. When Deo realizes what he has done, he understands he has forgotten his song. He asks himself, "How will I remember it?" One by one, the people of the village stop what they are doing, surround Deo, and begin singing his song to him. The song reminds Deo that he is a protector and not an aggressor.

When Deo's community sang his song back to him, their voices were the bassline of the shared rhythm of his life; he couldn't remember his song without them. The practice of rhythm is about listening for the shared rhythm of the universe, remembering your song, and learning to play it—for your own joy and for the healing of the world. This is deeply soulful work that will require ruthless honesty and zero tolerance for being "close enough." If a jazz musician can feel so connected to the rhythm that she can expose her soul through her improvised solo, you can, too. But the rhythm of your life must allow you to expose your soul by telling your honest story, using whatever instrument is yours. When the rhythm of your life forces you to live a lie instead of exposing your soul, you'll need to get back in sync with the rhythm of the universe so you can remember your song.

We all need getting back in sync with the rhythm of the universe because we all lose the beat from time to time. Jacob, in the Bible, needed a divine dream to wake him up to the reality that he had manipulated the rhythm of his family so he could realize the true rhythm telling him he wasn't alone after all. My friend Nick needed to stop wasting time on his smartphone so he could get back to inventing cool stuff. Even the *Zombie Apocalypse Guy* needed Jesus to see the fragile human being hidden underneath his brute strength and midnight wailing so he could stop trying to find a life among the dead. Does the rhythm of your life allow you to remember your song or does it keep you from remembering it?

· ● ·

Where Does Your Story Start?

Like jazz musicians that express their life story through improvisations in a shared song, we can express our own lives through words and through the stories we tell. When I sit down with someone for the first time, I often ask them to tell me their story. The way they start telling me their story usually reveals whether the rhythm of their life is helping them remember their song or is keeping them from remembering it.

If I didn't know anything about you, how would you choose to start telling me your story? Few people realize they get to choose where their story starts. A good story isn't just a collection of facts presented in tidy chronological order. It has a rhythm to it, where delicious characters with family secrets make questionable decisions, and it all slowly builds to an inevitable conflict and, finally, a satisfying resolution. If you pay attention to really good stories, you'll find sentences that reveal secrets like threads longing to be pulled. We're all longing for a safe place to tell our secrets, and we're all looking for someone who'll pull that thread.

Gail Honeyman gives us tantalizing threads to pull in her wonderful novel, *Eleanor Oliphant Is Completely Fine*, about a thirty-year-old English woman named Eleanor, who lives alone, doesn't have any friends, and is convinced the rhythm of her life is exactly as it should be, thank you very much, until she realizes it really, really isn't. When the story begins, the only person with whom she speaks regularly (*outside of work*) is her mother, who calls her once a week from prison. It takes most of the book for Eleanor to realize she doesn't know much about her own story. However, readers are let in on a huge part of it in chapter 1: "I have always taken great pride in managing my life alone. I'm a sole survivor—I'm Eleanor Oliphant. I don't need anyone else—there's no big hole in my life, no missing part of my own particular puzzle." A sentence like that reveals a secret but also keeps the cards really close to the vest. A sentence like that makes you wonder what kind of pain she's experienced, and if you'll ever get a chance to see her cards face up.

When you experience pain in the early chapters of your life, you can be reticent to show your cards to anyone. One of my friends is an adult son of a chronic alcoholic. He recently sent me a picture of a sheet of paper with the headline, "Characteristics and Personality Traits of an Adult Child of an Alcoholic." Underneath the picture, my friend wrote, "Sometimes therapy homework sucks." It appears unlikely that his dad will ever help my friend remember his song, and he won't ever be able to erase the ongoing pain of that loss. But that pain isn't the only true thing about him, and it doesn't have to be the defining sentence of the story he's now writing. He's become the kind of friend who's really good at helping me pull my cards away from the vest. His gentle questions convince me it's okay to tell him my secrets.

Great pain allows us to see how we are connected to each other and helps us keep in time with the rhythm of the universe and remember our song. Rachel Naomi Remen, founder of the Remen Institute for the Study of Health and Illness, believes a life well lived includes seeing how your wounds and weaknesses complete your identity, rather than keep you from living well. Understanding story, not facts, she says, is the only way to make sense of the complexity of life. She's also a physician who has lived with Crohn's disease for more than fifty years. In an interview with Krista Tippett, Remen said, "I have had Crohn's disease for fifty-two years. I've had eight major surgeries. But that doesn't tell you about my journey and what's happened to me because of that, and what it means to live with an illness like this and discover the power of being a human being."

Maybe you've lived with a disease or a disability for so long that you don't believe you can choose a different rhythm for your life. Maybe you can't hear your song because you haven't yet been shown what's deep inside of you and all around you, which might help you discover possibility again. When you realize you're telling your story using defining sentences that feel overly limiting, that's a great invitation to listen for something bigger. Sometimes discovering your real story can save your life.

• • ⬢ • •

An Origin Story

Have you ever asked someone where their story started? Has anyone ever asked you that question? If you tried to answer it, how far back would you go? Growing up, we had this white foldaway couch. My parents took great delight in letting me know—over and over again—that I was conceived on that couch (*thank you, Harold and Claudia*). But my story goes back way farther than that. It goes all the way back to when ordinary dust first met divine breath.

A few years ago, I attended a lecture given by Jim Bear Jacobs, a member of the Mohican Nation. In his lecture, he read Genesis 1 and then asked, "What do you notice about this creation story?" It was like a trick question that nobody wanted to get wrong, so nobody said anything. He gave us a hint: "Who's telling that story?" Again, silence.

"We love this story," he said, "especially us men, because it is dripping with testosterone. It is embedded in masculinity. In Genesis 1, we have a God who speaks, and things happen! What man wouldn't love that story?" He paced as he talked, and his cadence was slow and purposeful.

"What we can't glean from just reading this story is the historical context. Genesis 1 is written as a response to the Babylonian occupation and exile. In the Babylonian pantheon of gods, there are gods represented by animal sculptures and one that rides across the sky in his chariot of fire, the sun. Genesis 1 is a counternarrative: your gods are represented by animals, but our God said a word, and all animals came into existence. Your god rides on a chariot of fire, the sun, but our God created the sun. Our God is more powerful than your gods. This is a very masculine story, told by a masculine storyteller."

I leaned forward. I had never heard anyone talk like this before. His eyes twinkled before he said the next bit. "Genesis 1 is a powerful story," he said, "but I would suggest it's not our true beginning. It's not our origin story. If you want to read our true beginning, you have to turn the page to Genesis chapter 2. This, I suggest, is the indigenous creation story. It reads like you're sitting around the fire and listening to grandma speak. In Genesis 2, the Creator reaches down into the earth and pulls humanity out of the earth. In Genesis 2, the Creator gets her hands dirty during the work of creation. This is a motherly picture of God, in contrast to the patriarchal view of Genesis 1."

Listening, I remembered the birth of our three boys. I remembered the pain Mary experienced. I remembered the caring hands and voices of our midwives. It was messy, beautiful, and intimate—miraculous.

"And then the Creator bends down and breathes into the nostrils the breath of life—" Suddenly Jim Bear stopped, as if interrupting himself, to ask a question. "Why the nostrils? If you were giving CPR to someone, wouldn't you breathe into their mouth?" We were transfixed; we didn't even attempt to answer. We just wanted to hear him keep talking.

"When a baby is born, sometimes they have mucus plugs in their nostrils, and the only way to get them out is to suck them out. The creation story in the second chapter of Genesis is told by Mother God, and in this story, creation emerges only after a midwife reaches inside of her and pulls creation out. Our origin story is that we were midwifed by God, and the very breath of God was breathed into our nostrils."

I can't remember how Jim Bear's lecture ended, but I will never forget how radical it felt to have our origin story reframed by his observations on Genesis 1 and Genesis 2, and I began to see Genesis 1 as a powerful, necessary story. But Genesis 2 became an intimate story, connecting my very existence to divine nurture. To see my story starting with God as the midwife to my own birth is an utter contrast to a story in which God is shown as more powerful than other gods. When I can imagine the breath of God filling my lungs before I took my first breath, I am filled with hope that I can continue to find God wherever I am.

The rhythm of the universe is the divine heartbeat that is, right at this very moment, pulsing within all of creation—every proton and peach tree and, yes, every person—creating a rhythm that will someday result in one unified chorus. This is where everything is going, current events notwithstanding. The cynical, xenophobic vitriol that is topping the charts these days is vapor. The bait that keeps being taken every time either "side" is demonized will one day go out of stock forever. The irrevocable and unstoppable direction of the universe is guided by a shared story that is infused with hope and driven forward by love.

● ● ● ● ●

Practice: Tapping along with the Rhythm of Mystery

Sometimes rekindling our faith requires participating in sacred rituals that help us stay in time with the rhythm of the universe when the vitriol drowns it out. Something like that happened to my sister Lisa, an Episcopal priest who leads a parish in South Minneapolis. She found her calling well into the middle of her life, during a frustrating season when she couldn't remember her song. Out of the blue, she heard it again after wandering into a church and receiving the bread

and wine of the Eucharist. "You aren't bad," she heard Someone whisper that day. "You're just starving. Stay and eat."

I don't know what it is about the bread and wine of
the Eucharist in our family. I guess we're just hungry for it,
because it affects me, too.

Participating in a weekly rhythm of celebrating the
Eucharist connects me to the rhythm of the universe and
helps me remember my song. The seating arrangement of
the church where I worship consists of four sections of pews,
each section the same size. The Eucharist table rests at the
intersection of all four sections of pews, in the exact center of
the congregation. I always sit in a front pew. Every Sunday
morning, the person presiding begins the Eucharistic liturgy
with a brief call and response: "The Lord be with you," she
calls out. "And, also with you," we respond. There is a grace-
ful rhythm to these first words of the ritual, an equanimity
that allows the room to exhale. Each phrase has five syllables,
which perfectly matches the time it takes for one breath in
(*The Lord be with you*); and for one breath out (*And also with
you*). That's a pretty good way for the church to start whatever story it's trying to tell.

Then she invites us to "lift up [our] hearts." What does
it mean to lift up your heart? I place my hands over my own
heart, trying to feel its rhythm. "It's courageous," I think
to myself, "to lift up your heart." What if all my secrets and
fears fall out? I think of my friend with an eating disorder,

sitting on the other side of the center aisle, a few rows back from me. She's in and out of church because she's in and out of treatment. How is her heart? Does she need help lifting it up? I think about my friend who sneaks in after the service has already begun. He hasn't really gotten over the divorce, and his kids aren't really talking to him. Can a broken heart be lifted up? I think about my transgender, bisexual friend who comes to church when he's home from college. Neither the queer community nor the church has been a safe place for him to lift up his heart—or any other part of his body, for that matter. Yet each week, the motley lot of us are invited to lift up our hearts. Is that why we receive the Eucharist together instead of alone? Perhaps seeing others lift up their hearts gives you courage to lift up yours. We respond together, "We lift them up to the Lord." That statement has seven syllables, a rhythm that stretches a normal breath to its limit.

"Let us give thanks to the Lord our God," says the presider. We respond quickly, as if we're afraid of getting caught in a lie, "It is right to give God thanks and praise." I crack a tiny, imperceptible smile. I confess I don't always agree. Sometimes it is right to give God a piece of your mind.

The Words of Institution are next: "On the night he was handed over to suffering and death, our Lord Jesus Christ took the bread; and when he had given thanks to you, he broke it . . . ." My mind usually wanders during this part. I yawn and rub the back of my neck. I hear the small but satisfying snap of a cap going back on its marker as one of my boys finishes whatever he's been drawing. "Therefore, we proclaim the mystery of faith. Christ has died, Christ is risen, Christ will come again." Suddenly I'm back in the room, feeling glad these institutional words call faith a mystery. I walk down the pew toward the center aisle. I turn right and get in line to receive Communion. I look up to the balcony, and I see the Christ, his stained-glass skin backlit by the sun, casting a rainbow of color over the congregation.

When I arrive at the Communion table, I receive a small piece of bread. I look into familiar eyes and hear familiar words: "The body of Christ, broken for you; take and eat. The blood of Christ, shed for you; take and drink." I dip the bread into the cup with my right hand. My left hand reflexively comes underneath my right hand, forming a cup to catch any drips. "Amen," I say with a slight head nod. I place the body and blood into my mouth, slowly chewing and swallowing. I turn right and walk toward the outer wall. I turn right again and walk along the outside aisle to my pew in the front. I sit down. Did I experience anything in that moment? Did anything really change in how I see myself? Did anything change in how I see the world?

Christ has died, Christ is risen, Christ will come again. I suppose you could turn those into fighting words, but I don't think you're supposed to *defend* mystery. I don't even think you're supposed to *believe* mystery. Maybe you can only hope to participate in it, trying your best to hear mystery's rhythm and tap your foot along to the beat. Maybe if you do that long enough, you'll remember your song.

If you regularly receive the Eucharist, I invite you to participate in it mindfully. That doesn't mean you should waste a second trying to work up guilt about your sins. Sins have a way of providing their own punishment, and you've probably suffered enough already. To participate in the Eucharist mindfully means to linger long enough to remember that the entire cosmos is being remade in that bread and wine and to hold out hope that even the worst of enemies can be turned into the best of friends, as when water was turned into wine.

A piece of bread isn't just a piece of bread.

A cup of wine isn't just a cup of wine.

Thich Nhat Hanh wrote, "This is exactly what Jesus was trying to overcome when he said *This is My body. This is My blood.* When we are truly there, dwelling deeply in the present moment, we can see that the bread and the wine are really the Body and the Blood of Christ and the priest's words are truly the words of the Lord. The Body of Christ is the body of God, the body of ultimate reality, the ground of all existence. We do not have to look anywhere else for it. It resides deep in our own being."

If you do not receive the Eucharist or aren't in the Christian tradition, be at peace. The church doesn't own the Communion table. It is on loan from Jesus, whose table is neither Christian nor Jewish nor even particularly religious. If the rhythm of the Eucharist isn't something you celebrate, remember to mindfully participate in your own rhythm(s), where that irrevocable and unstoppable direction of the universe is guided by a shared story, infused with hope and driven forward by love.

If your story starts with God midwifing your own birth, perhaps it can continue that way, too, every time something new needs to come to life from deep within you. If God filled your lungs before you took your first breath, God continues to fill your lungs with divine breath with every inhalation and exhalation. God really is hiding inside you, with each breath.

That's a song with rhythm. ⬡

⸱ ● ⬡ ● ⸱

Study the Stone

Be yourself. And if what this means
is unclear to you, look around at

the things of this earth. Study the stone
which always does what it was made

to do: it doesn't always fall in the
same way, sometimes resting in high

places and at other times finding its
rest where the earth allows it to lie,

but its purpose is to move downward,
and in this the stone loves God in the

way it can, singing the new song
which God gives each creature and thing—

and also you who read this and at times
wonder what to do and how to be.

PRACTICE

Conversation

To be present with those I consider "other," I practice
conversation: learning to ask—and answer—questions that
continually expand how I see and understand the world.

If you want to reveal how insufferably self-righteous you
can be *(and why wouldn't you?),* all you need to do is try
to have a conversation about God with someone from your
own religious tradition with whom you disagree. Progres-
sive or conservative or somewhere in between, we're all the
same: we love being right, and we hate when that rightness
is threatened.

A few years ago, I had a fight on Facebook with an old
friend named Tom. I had posted something to which Tom
took offense, implying I'd painted a group of people with
brushstrokes a little too broadly. I'd recently promised myself

to be a little less polite on Facebook, so I fired back a comment designed to win instead of listen. After a few heated exchanges, our mutual friend Steve jumped into the conversation and suggested that the three of us meet face-to-face to understand each other better. I had zero interest in meeting, so I closed my laptop and moved on.

Later, I changed my mind. Tom and I met for lunch at one of those massive restaurants that serve waffle fries and thirty-six-ounce beers. When Tom told me about his parents and his childhood and also about the challenges he'd faced while trying to raise his own family, my shoulders dropped. It's one thing to argue with a one-dimensional avatar on social media; it's another to listen to a human being with a story that includes pain, disappointment, and hope. I left that lunch feeling hopeful. I don't have to agree with everything Tom believes—or anything at all, for that matter—to honor his story and simply listen. I don't have to defend my "rightness" in order to hold a deep conviction. And anyway, being an asshole and being polite are not the only two options for how to have conversations.

In *Conjectures of a Guilty Bystander*, Thomas Merton writes about the universal human desire to possess "the truth." But none of us, Merton suggests, is actually that virtuous. We don't really want the truth. We really just want to be "in the right":

What we seek is not the pure truth but the partial truth that justifies our prejudices, our limitations, our selfishness. This is not "the truth." It is only an argument strong enough to prove us "right." And usually our desire to be right is correlative to our conviction that somebody else (perhaps everybody else) is wrong. Why do we want to prove them wrong? Because we need them to be wrong. For if they are wrong, and we are right, then our untruth becomes truth: our selfishness becomes justice and virtue: our cruelty and lust cannot be fairly condemned. We can rest secure in the fiction we have determined to embrace as "truth."

If you only search for ways to strengthen an argument for what you already believe, your faith will burn down to embers and eventually die out, even if you think it's burning brightly. But if you have the courage to keep searching for better questions that expand the way you believe in God, your faith will spark to new life over and over again.

How do we learn to understand each other and be understood? How do we learn to ask questions that continually expand how we see the world? How do we resist the temptation to caricature people with whom we disagree or whose decisions we don't understand?

In Yogic thought, there are ten jewels designed to help people live well. The first five jewels (*the Yamas*) come from a Sanskrit word meaning restraint: nonviolence, truthfulness, non-stealing, non-excess, and non-possessiveness. The last five jewels (*the Niyamas)* are observances: purity, contentment, self-discipline, self-study, and surrender. Nonviolence is the first jewel because it's the foundation on which all the other jewels rest. Without nonviolence, the rest are impossible to practice. Nonviolence simply means to do no harm. Jesus said it this way: *Love your enemies, pray for those who curse you.*

Sometimes it's obvious when we're doing harm to ourselves or others, but most of the time, it's hard to tell. My friend Dava is a forty-two-year-old married mother of two high school kids who lives in North Minneapolis and who also happened to feel an irresistible invitation—maybe even a calling—to attend a three-year program at Union Theological Seminary in New York City. When she started talking to family and friends about the possibility, she quickly found out that even in 2019, wives and mothers aren't supposed to do stuff like that. Some expressed shock that she would even consider it. How would she maintain her marriage and her relationship with her children while living so far away? Weren't there other seminary options closer to home? Isn't that particular seminary really . . . different? Every time I talked to her about it, she had a new story about someone else telling her she shouldn't go without even listening to the reasons why she felt maybe she should. She told me how hard it was to trust her deep inner sense of calling, in light of criticism from people who were close to her. Those people had done harm to Dava, though not intentionally. It wasn't necessarily harmful to question whether or not she should go, but it was harmful to weigh in without taking the time to really listen. And maybe Dava did harm to herself by inviting certain people to weigh in on such a tender and important process.

Why is it that so many conversations about faith involve foolish questions designed to trap us into giving foolish answers? Is it possible to change the tone of these conversations so they're less defensive and more expansive? Why do we mistrust any experience of the divine that feels unfamiliar to our own experience? What new experiences of God do we miss when we insist on keeping our old ones on repeat?

● ● ◆ ● ●

Practice: Learning to Ask Better Questions

Do we really shine like the sun when we'd rather leave some people in the shadows? If we want to have better conversations that lead to expanding how we see and understand the world, we need to learn to ask questions, ones that invite people to expand rather than defend their territories. Jesus was particularly good at asking expansive questions and inviting people to expand their territories. The questions weren't always comfortable, and he wasn't always polite. He also knew how to refuse to answer dead-end questions by dangling different questions, ones that would lead people somewhere new, hoping they'd bite (*not everyone did*).

The parable of the Good Samaritan is a good example of the kinds of questions Jesus asked and also the kinds of questions he refused to answer. First of all, parables aren't cute stories; they're purposely confusing and hard to follow. They're tricky, but they're not traps. They're designed with layers of meaning, which allow you to expand as far as you're capable of expanding. Parables are like those wooden Russian *matryoshka* dolls of decreasing size, which are placed one inside of the other. When you open one of them up, you find another one inside of it. Parables contain juxtaposition and paradox, which give listeners a choice: Will they keep opening up the next doll to find what else is there, or will they stop? Parables are essentially great questions constructed with characters and a plot, where you get to choose the ending based on how far you want to take it.

Jesus told the parable of the Good Samaritan after a religious leader asked Jesus what he needed to do to inherit eternal life. Jesus responded by asking him what the law says. The religious leader answered quickly and correctly, "Love the

Lord your God with all your heart and with all your soul and with all your strength. And love your neighbor as yourself."

"Correct answer," Jesus said. "Do that and you will live." But the religious leader wasn't satisfied. He pressed Jesus with what on the surface might have sounded like a good question: "But who is my neighbor?"

That's a tricky question. Is it sincere, or is it designed to reinforce his already-established territory? Instead of answering that tricky question, Jesus told a parable to help the religious leader see what kind of question he'd just asked.

Here's the gist of the parable: A man was left for dead by the side of the road after being robbed. A priest and a Levite passed by the man without helping him, but a Samaritan stopped to bandage the man's wounds and then took him to an inn, where he left money for the man's room and board and doctor's bills, promising to come back in a few days. When Jesus finished telling the story, he asked the religious leader a question with more layers than I can count: "Which of the three men was a neighbor to the man who was robbed?"

"The one who showed him mercy," the religious leader answered. How many layers did he understand? Did he see what Jesus was trying to show him? Do we?

We think the priest and Levite are insufferable hypocrites for refusing to help the guy who was left for dead, but you could also argue they were loving God and loving people by remaining ritually pure so they could offer sacrifices at the temple later that day. If priests and Levites abandoned ritual purity laws, the whole temple system would fall apart. You could argue they were correct in doing what they did; they were just following the laws of their religious tribe. It's a little too moralistic to infer that Jesus's main point was that the priest and Levite should have done anything differently. There's something deeper going on.

Most religious leaders in the time of Jesus saw Samaritans the way Draco Malfoy saw mudbloods (*in the Harry Potter books, an offensive term for wizards who have non-wizard parents*). When Jesus asked the religious leader "which of the three men" was a neighbor to the man who was robbed, he was inviting the religious leader to see the Samaritan man in the same class of human being as the priest and the Levite, which expanded the conversation in an extremely unpredictable direction. If priests and Levites can love God and neighbor by showing mercy to temple worshippers by offering sacrifices, Samaritans can love God and neighbor by tending to people who are left for dead by the side of the road.

"What must I do to inherit eternal life?" is a fair question, but a question like that usually leads to either/or answers, which entrench fear. In contrast, "To whom can you show mercy?" is a question that can take the conversation in many unpredictable directions, expanding the way we see and understand the world. The parable of the Good Samaritan isn't about doing nice things for strangers, it's about expanding an either/or category to both/and.

Asking better questions isn't a guarantee that the other person will participate, but it might lead to a surprising interaction where both parties expand their understanding of the world. In short, it could open up a conversation that might help you rekindle your faith, which isn't a bad way to spend a day. ●

· ● ● ● ·

Practice: Learning to Request a Different Question

Sometimes we'll be on the receiving end of a dead-end question, and unless we're content with freezing up, setting our own trap, or running away, we'll need to find a different way to respond. We won't always become aware soon enough, but when we do, we can pause long enough to make a mindful choice about how we want to request a different question.

During my favorite class in college—my senior seminar course in sociology—I read a book that introduced me to a new way to respond to a dead-end question. On the first day of class, our professor (*who looked a lot like a young Sam Shepard*) told us that our entire grade would be based on our ability to engage in thoughtful conversation and discussion in class based on the assigned reading. There would be no papers and no tests. One of the books we read was *Zen and the Art of Motorcycle Maintenance* by Robert Pirsig, which introduced me to a Japanese word, *mu*, which literally means *no thing*. *Mu* is a response equal to but different from yes and no, capable of refusing dualistic categories expanding one's understanding in an unpredictable direction. *Mu* is a response you might give to a question that only has room for an either/or answer when you want the conversation to expand beyond those limitations. *Mu* allows you to say that giving a yes or no answer to a particular question would be to dishonor the subject matter.

Mu was reincarnated for me when recently I listened to a podcast featuring Pádraig Ó Tuama, a gentle, brilliant writer, poet, and mystic from Ireland. Pádraig is also gay, and he grew up in the kind of Christianity where being gay went far beyond the limits of acceptability. During the interview, Pádraig defined *mu* as a request to un-ask a question that was designed to categorize as an either/or something that shouldn't be categorized that way. A gay poet and spiritual teacher from Ireland probably has many opportunities each day to use *mu*. "Un-ask the question," Pádraig explained, "because there is a better question to be asked. Asking a wiser question might unfold us into asking even more wiser questions, whereas certain kinds of questions just entrench fear."

Questions that entrench fear don't have to be dead ends. *Mu* allows you to at least request that the conversation expand beyond fear and into unpredictable directions. Your body usually knows first when you're being asked a dead-end question. You might feel uneasy in your gut or your shoulders, as if you are being trapped. Instead of answering the dead-end question, you can pause and find a way to request a different question by asking one of the following questions:

- Why do you ask?
- Before I answer, may I ask a few questions?
- I'm not sure my answer to that question is going to help, so I'd rather not answer it. Can you ask that question in a different way? ●

· ● ● ● ·

Practice: Receiving Wise Questions

Of course, not all questions we receive are dead ends. When someone asks us a wise question, it can help us start moving in a better direction. Sometimes a wise question can give us permission to let go of the trapeze that got you "here" so you can grab ahold of the trapeze that will help you get where you want to go. Learning to receive wise questions helps us see things about ourselves we might otherwise overlook.

It was a little embarrassing, but I received a great question during a pickup basketball game when I was in my early thirties. It was my first time playing with these guys, most of whom were around my age, but there was one guy who didn't seem to belong. He was short, round, and old (*I don't mean to pile on, but he also wasn't a very good at basketball player*). But he was vocal on the court, and people listened to him. Every time I came, the old guy was always there. After missing more than a few jump shots one week, I came off the court and found myself standing next to the old guy on the sidelines.

"I can't believe my shots aren't falling," I complained.

"Have you practiced at all between last week and this week?" he asked. I shook my head. I hadn't even thought of practicing.

"Well, then," he said, "you should be completely satisfied with your performance today."

Snap.

I'm not sure if he ever read *Zen and the Art of Motorcycle Maintenance*, but he was a master of *mu*. Because of one wise question, I realized I wasn't the basketball player I used to be, and if I wanted to get better again, it would take hard work and lots of practice. His question also helped me realize

I didn't really care about basketball anymore. I didn't go back to that pickup game, and I don't think I've played any competitive basketball since. And I'm one hundred percent fine with that. ●

· ● ● ● ·

Practice: Letting Go

We've explored the first Yama (*restraint*), which is non-violence, the practice of doing no harm. The last Yama is non-possessiveness. We can think of non-possessiveness as learning to experience the real pleasures of life— receiving a hug, enjoying a sunset, or wasting time with the Divine—by letting go of the ways we tend to overvalue our material possessions. But I think it can be even more challenging to let go of certainty. If we think of non-possessiveness as learning to experience the real pleasures of a diverse world—learning from an imam if you're a Christian, losing an argument but gaining a friend, or changing your mind about a cherished belief—we'll find ourselves slowly being less defensive and more curious. Giving up the right to be right takes courage and humility, but once you do, your conversations will lead to such breathtaking vistas that demanding to be right will eventually feel like being locked in prison.

This may sound overly simplistic, but we can eventually learn to give up the right to be right by letting go of small, habitual attachments that we don't even see as attachments. If you're the kind of person who orders the same thing every time you go to your favorite restaurant, consider letting someone else order for you the next time you go. If doing so makes you feel anxious, that club sandwich on toasted wheat bread cut in triangles, hold the bacon, has a hold on you. If it didn't, you'd be fine ordering something else. That's how attachment works; what you hold onto holds onto you, even if it's just a sandwich.

When we keep doing the same things over and over again without thinking, we aren't living mindfully. But when we stop and consider doing something different, we're mindfully letting go of an attachment. What small attachments can you let go of so you can eventually learn to let go of your need to be right?

- Get a totally different drink at the coffee shop every day for a week.
- Pick an article of clothing you have more than one of, and get rid of all the extras until you have only one left—one hoodie, one jacket, or even one pair of shoes if you feel extra radical.
- Stop to ask for directions instead of using GPS to get somewhere you need to go.

One of the best opportunities to give up the right to be right is when you notice you're getting defensive. When that familiar feeling of anger rises up and you find yourself shutting down, interrupting, or overexplaining your motives, stop and breathe. As you follow your breath in and out, you can ask yourself a question: What am I trying to defend?

Don't judge your answers as they come up; just notice them. See if you can consciously choose to let go of anything. See how it feels to simply stop arguing your case. This will take a long time to learn, and sometimes you'll be so triggered you can't stop. That's okay. Just keep noticing.

Wasting our time defending ourselves is like those stupid monkeys who reach through the narrow bars to grab a banana and eventually get trapped there because they just won't let go. We can keep holding onto being right and eventually get trapped there forever, or we can choose to give up our right to be right and be free. When we learn to give up our right to be right, we'll expand the way we see and understand the world in profound ways.

May you learn to have conversations that expand the way you see and understand the world. May those conversations lead you to expanding your view of God, yourself, and everybody else—who, after all is said and done, really are shining like the sun, whether you can see it or not, and whether they know it or not.

And may the *mu* be with you. ●

Behind You

There is a wanting of God
so much
that you are willing
to forsake everything
godly to find him.
Ponder this,
The God who is beyond
what is godly.
Know this,
that you may have to leave
more than you ever imagined
behind.

Delight

To be truly alive with what I am doing, I practice delight:
learning to fully receive whatever is in front of me.

When I was twenty-one years old, I tasted grace so real
I wept and couldn't stop weeping. It was a conversion
though, according to the ledger of my church experience,
I'd already been converted quite a few times. I'm genuinely
grateful for it, but the church I grew up attending gave lots of
opportunities to be converted, just in case the last one didn't
quite take (*and maybe that's what made this new taste of grace
so necessary*). Here's what happened: Just after I tasted the
bread and wine (*okay, it was grape juice*) of Communion,
God whispered, "I like you." Just that, nothing else. Well, it
wrecked me. For a person who had made dozens of serious
decisions about God, this delightful gift of grace was buried

treasure. Since then, I've let go of a lot, and I've grabbed hold of quite a few new things, but that mystical experience led me to experience the God who really was eternally waiting for me with love. Practicing delight leads you to *experience* the goodness of God, rather than just making decisions about the goodness of God.

Practicing delight—learning to receive whatever is in front of you—starts by refusing to slice life into categories. You don't have a spiritual life; your whole life is spiritual.

· · ⬡ · ·

Practice: Receiving Life as a Gift

Delight is your unconscious response to something you find enjoyable. Delight leaves you feeling full of wonder (*wonderfull*). With practice, you can learn to delight in almost anything, but you need tutors, which can pop up anywhere, sometimes even in baggage claim.

The rest of us were bleary eyed and slimy skinned, waiting for our luggage in the hell that is commercial air travel, uncomfortably close proximity with complete strangers while being forced to wait longer to get somewhere better. But there was this kid who was maybe eighteen months old. Each and every time a bag tumbled from the conveyor belt onto the carousel, this kid erupted with laughter—head-thrown-back, eyes-shut, straight-up howling. Because *luggage*. Pretty soon, everyone was laughing, as if we'd flown all that way just to watch luggage tumble down that carousel.

Sometimes a cup of coffee with a friend can fill you with wonder. "Watch this," my friend said, unable to contain his excitement. He had ordered a large Americano to be served in a clear pint glass, with cream on the side. When his coffee arrived, he poured a little bit of that snow-white cream into that pitch-black Americano. As the cream danced and twirled down into the bottom of the glass, I laughed out loud. When I looked up, he was looking right into my eyes, smiling his silly, dopey, masterful smile.

Where do you experience delight? Maybe it's the feeling of your body moving on an early-morning run or a gentle walk at night. Maybe it's when you're exploring a new city or hiking in the mountains. Maybe it's when people you love accomplish an important task. Maybe it's the smell of dirt and rain in springtime after a long winter. Maybe it's painting or sculpting or cooking or photography that leaves you feeling full of wonder.

Whether it's mowing the lawn, listening to music, setting a table full of your favorite foods or being on a large body of water surrounded by your best friends, practicing delight— receiving whatever's in front of you as a gift—includes those things but also goes *beyond* those things. Your morning walk *is* delightful, those mountains *really are* beautiful, and your best friends really *are* great. But when your experiences of delight are limited to preplanned activities you get to do when you're finished with the annoying responsibilities of life, you'll miss out on a lot of gifts. And anyway, those preplanned activities will probably need to get bigger and bigger in order for you to keep responding with delight. Pretty soon, you'll need to be surrounded by your best friends, on a boat, *accompanied by several dozen dolphins.*

In the first chapter, I mentioned that the journey of rekindling your faith won't be like looking for a needle in a haystack. That's especially true when we're talking about delight. Sure, delight is what bursts out of you when your best friend flies across the country for your fiftieth birthday party without telling you. But if you can't sometimes choke with laughter at luggage or marvel at the way cream dances in your coffee, you'll end up yawning even when dolphins do jump over the bow of your boat. It's easy to feel delighted when you find the needle, but if you can also take delight in everything you find while searching for the needle, all of life will be a gift.

The student is delighted when she finally finds a needle in the haystack, but the student becomes a master when she learns to see a haystack as a delightful opportunity to take a nap. And when she wakes up, she laughs out loud, marveling at the simple and surprising pleasure of sleeping on a haystack. "Surely the Lord was in this haystack," she says, "and I was not aware of it." The mindful practice of delight is learning to find pleasure in whatever's in front of you, even if your boss is kicking your ass in a crowded conference room (*he probably looks ridiculous with that vein popping out of his forehead*).

If we want to learn to see all of life—even the unexpected and painful twists and turns—as a gift, we'll need to learn how to delight in time itself. If we can't learn to see time differently, our lives will end up feeling like the airport: a series of unexpected delays while you're waiting to go somewhere better.

The Greeks had two different ways of understanding time: *chronos* and *kairos*. *Chronos* (*the source of the word chronological*) is clock time. When you're operating with *chronos*, you have to pay attention to expiration dates, appointments, and how long it's going to take to drive to your three o'clock meeting. *Chronos* is measured, and it always marches forward without stopping for anything, second by second, minute by minute, hour by hour, day by day, year by year. It turns out, you don't kill time, it kills you.

If *chronos* measures seconds, *kairos* measures moments. *Kairos* refers to that opportune moment when something new is possible, and you are invited to participate. A *kairos* moment is when something is ripe for the picking. A life with *kairos* would be a love affair.

You can't live without *chronos*; you still need to be on time for work and take the garbage cans out every other Tuesday. But you don't have to spend your life serving *chronos*. It doesn't have to kill you. If you do choose to spend your life serving *chronos*, you'll always be punching the clock, whether you're earning money for it or not. Time will be something you'll try to save, kill, or steal. But if you choose to look for *kairos* to show up even while you're working the late shift or waiting for the bus, you might experience the gift of a stranger's kindness or a significant conversation with a coworker. You might even find the God who's eternally waiting for you with love.

Lenny Duncan describes his own *kairos* moment in his beautiful and challenging book, *Dear Church: A Love Letter from a Black Preacher to the Whitest Denomination in the U.S.* Duncan, a queer, black pastor in a very white denomination, says he "was more likely to end up in prison than the pulpit. In fact, it's a miracle I'm still alive. I'm a former drug dealer, sex worker, homeless queer teen, and felon. How the hell did I get here?" Lenny met God at church, when the pastor serving Communion (*there it is again*) said, "This is Jesus's table; he made no restrictions, and neither do we." Lenny writes, "I was smitten immediately. There was no member-ship meeting, no checking my theology, no 'friendly' talk with the pastor before I approached the table of grace. I was welcome, and this was revolutionary to me."

Not every moment explodes with new life, but you'll miss the ones that do unless you learn to delight in time. And when you learn to delight in time, you might be surprised at how many moments actually are exploding with new life.

Thich Nhat Hanh addresses this in his classic book, *The Miracle of Mindfulness*, where he writes, "All time is my time." The book begins with the story of a man who came to visit Thich Naht Hanh and told him about a dis-

> Not every moment explodes with new life, but you'll miss the ones that do unless you learn to delight in time. ●

covery he had made that changed the way he saw his demanding life with his wife, their two young children, and all of his other responsibilities:

"I've discovered a way to have a lot more time," the man said.

"In the past, I used to look at my life as if it were divided into several parts. One part I reserved for Joey (his son), another part was for Sue (his wife), another part to help with Ana (his newborn daughter), another part for household work. The time left I considered my own. I could read, write, do research, go for walks."

"But now I try not to divide my time into parts anymore. When I help Joey with his homework, I try to find ways of seeing his time as my own time. . . . The same with Sue. The remarkable thing is that now I have unlimited time for myself."

By learning to stop dividing time, he learned that *all time was his time.*

If that sounds a little like a Jedi mind trick, consider this: seeing your time as divided is just as much a construct as seeing all time as your time. It's *chronos* and *kairos*. You get to choose if you'll let Chronos slowly kill you or if you'll let Kairos give you a new lease on life. *Kairos* is sacred time; it's when you return to here to find God eternally waiting for you with love.

Rabbi Abraham Joshua Heschel understood time as *holy*. In his masterful book *The Sabbath*, he pointed out that the first thing to be called holy in the Hebrew Bible was not a place, a thing, or even a person, but *time* itself. Holiness in Hebrew doesn't mean pristine and virginal; it means to be set apart. When something is called holy in the Bible, it means it isn't like everything else, so you you're not supposed to treat it like everything else. For Heschel, time wasn't something to kill, save, waste, or endure; it was something to receive as a gift from God to the world. He saw time as a synonym for the way creation continually regenerates itself. "Every instant is an act of creation," Heschel wrote. "A moment is not a terminal but a flash, a signal of Beginning. Time is perpetual innovation, a synonym for continuous creation. Time is God's gift to the world of space."

When we make the choice to be present to the moment in front of us, rather than choosing to see it as an arrival or a waiting area, we delight in that moment by honoring its holiness. The more we learn to receive whatever is in front of us, the more we'll feel the Great Midwife breathing into our nostrils the breath of new life. ●

· ○ ● ○ ·

Practice: Honoring the Holiness of This Moment

Unless you work the night shift or just choose to sleep until two in the afternoon, you probably do certain things every morning to get ready to do other things a little later that morning—say, work, school, or caring for an elderly parent. Whatever the details of our situation, each of us gets to choose how to see and participate in each of those moments.

Here's how it works. After you've set an intention to honor the holiness of each moment, you'll mostly forget about it. You'll start to notice how often you aren't honoring the holiness of any moment, and you'll be tempted to feel like a pathetic loser. *Please understand this:* mindfulness is the continual process of coming back to the present moment each time you realize you've left it. Each time you realize you've left the present moment, you're not failing—you're actually practicing mindfulness!

It's helpful to develop a familiar mantra or action that brings you back to the present without judging yourself for leaving it. When we become aware that we're rushing through a moment to get to the next one, we can stop, take a slow breath innnnn . . . and ouuut. Then we can smile, even if it's just a half smile. Then we can ask, "How can I honor this moment?" If that feels too wordy, you could simply bring to mind the image of *chronos*—a Grim Reaper—and gently tell him you'd rather not die today, thank you very much. We aren't forcing anything to happen that doesn't want to happen. We're just allowing each moment to be what it wants to be and to pass in its own time. We're just giving ourselves the opportunity to receive whatever is in front of us, so we can partner with that moment in case something new wants to be created.

Learning to receive whatever's in front of you is hard when you're busy thinking of things that aren't currently in front of you. When you take a shower, and you become aware that you're scanning your brain for all the things you need to get done that day, or you notice you're scrubbing your body like a teenager working at a car wash, you can ask yourself, "How can I honor the holiness of this moment?" You might choose to spend your shower slowly naming the parts of your body as you touch them, thanking each of them for the job they do. Or you could close your eyes and just enjoy the simple pleasure of warm water on your skin for an extra minute or two. That's participating in the creation of a new beginning.

When you drink that first cup of coffee in the morning, instead of drinking it as quickly as possible while you make breakfast or pack your lunch or drive to work, what if you asked yourself, "How can I honor the holiness of this moment?" If you sip your coffee and choose not to do anything else while sipping your coffee, you could close your eyes and try to identify the flavors you're tasting. What do you love about the taste of coffee? How do you feel as its warmth spreads through your body? Enjoying the pleasure of taste is receiving what's in front of you, and in doing so, you create a moment of gratitude.

Maybe as you climb into bed at night, you become aware that you're getting agitated while scrolling through your phone. That's your cue to ask: "How can I honor the holiness of this moment?" You might choose to place your phone in a different room at night, choosing to spend those first few minutes in bed scrolling through your day instead, recalling a few things for which you feel grateful, and spending a few quiet moments expressing that gratitude to the Divine.

And, yes, you'll mostly forget to return to the present, and you'll probably feel like an idiot when you do. But each time you do return to the present, you're creating new pathways for your brain to respond to familiar things in new ways. This is what delight is all about.

We can also practice honoring the holiness of this moment when we're with others. When we're going to meet a friend for lunch, we can ask ourselves how we'll honor the holiness of our time together. What will we do with our phones when we meet? One of my friends intentionally puts his phone away, never putting his phone on the table between us. By making this mindful choice, he honors our time together. Without words, he's saying the person in front of him and the conversation are important, and interruptions can wait. Maybe his phone is in his pocket or his car, or maybe it's even at home. This small act of kindness shows he delights in his time with others.

When we return home after being gone, others may be waiting for us. We can ask ourselves how we'll honor the holiness of arriving at home. If we live with other people or with pets, we can look each of them in the eyes and smile or maybe give them a hug. Who knows what new beginning might be created by this small choice? ⬡

· ⬡ ⬢ ⬡ ·

Practice: Learning to See Gifts Even in the Most Painful Moments

It's easy to learn to enjoy a delicious cup of coffee or to delight in the warmth of your dog lying next to you at night, but it's really hard to honor the holiness of the moment when you get fired, or when your doctor calls with scary test results, or when the person who promised to love you forever tells you that forever has turned out to be a little too long. I don't know how to delight in those things. I don't know if you even can delight in them without resorting to the *bullshittiest* of religious platitudes, like God being in control and God needing another angel in heaven and God not giving you more than you can handle. But it's possible to honor the holiness of those moments because they're not like all the other moments in your life. I do think it's possible for *kairos* to steal the show even when the Grim Reaper seems to be the star.

My family and I experienced a kairos moment in the weeks leading up to Mary's dad's death. James Miles Martin was a big man with a big laugh who grew up on a farm on the Mississippi River, riding horses and watching John Wayne movies. He remained a cowboy his whole life; he concealed and carried, sometimes even at his granddaughter's birthday parties. He had a scar shaped like a crescent moon just under his left eye from getting kicked in the face by a horse when he was a teenager. He loved food but was always trying to shave off a few pounds. He'd brag about being an international singer and then reveal he'd sung at a wedding in Canada *once*. His parents had provided for him but never once delighted in him, so gentleness wasn't a language he ever spoke with much fluency, but he loved his family with a loyalty as tough as leather. He was also one of the most generous people I've ever met; when times were tight for Mary and me, he'd quietly slip us an envelope filled with crisp hundred-dollar bills.

This past summer, he had two strokes and began slipping away fast. The evening after he stopped swallowing, the boys and I met Mary at the hospital to say good-bye to Jim. His skin was white and paper thin, and his long, straight fingers had turned yellowish. Mary wrapped her arms around the boys when we entered the room and told them that Poppa wouldn't wake up or open his eyes, but he'd understand what they said to him. Mary's mom was bending over him, her mouth pressed against his face, whispering whatever people whisper to each other when they've been married for almost sixty years, when they've buried secrets and treasures in the same private place that's about to be sealed forever.

We didn't tell the boys to go in order by age, but they did anyway. They each touched their Poppa on the arm and said good-bye.

"This is Isaac, Poppa. I love you. You can go now. It's okay."

Elijah quietly wiggled around Isaac, and when he spoke, his voice was just above a whisper. "Poppa, this is Lige. I love you. Good-bye."

Ben tried to touch his Poppa, but his tears beat him to the punch, so he buried his blond head in Mary's arms first. "I love you, Poppa. This is Ben."

Then it was my turn. What came out was mostly in croaks and squeaks, but I'm sure he understood. At some point, he reached out to me with both his arms, and I placed one of his hands on the scratchy stubble on my cheek as I said good-bye.

Chronos will have his pound of flesh; moments of delight can't stop death. But Kairos shows up when we honor the holiness of the moment when our fathers and grandfathers slip away from us; we'll carry the marks of those final touches forever. As the four of us—my boys and I—walked back to the parking garage together after our final good-bye to Jim, we cried big tears. We didn't say much, but we hung onto each other as we walked, our bodies whispering whatever fathers and sons whisper to each other when they are learning to speak the language of gentleness.

To be truly alive with what I am doing, I practice delight: learning to fully receive whatever is in front of me. Sometimes you can shine like the sun even when all the lights go out. ●

· · ● · ·

Your Only Delight

There is in me a radiance
that never ceases, and if

I had eyes to see into the
darkest depths of my heart

I would know that this inner
spark is all You ever see

of me, whether by day
or by night, and this

alone is my one and
Your only delight.

PRACTICE

Restoration

To be at one with all of creation, I practice restoration:
learning to welcome the weakness, fragility, and
loneliness in myself and others for our mutual healing.

Jesus once told a story about a gentle father who had
two sons, both of whom were lost in their own way. The
younger one left in search of faraway needles in unfamiliar
haystacks but returned home beaten up and broken down.
The way Jesus tells the story, the only thing that eclipsed the
father's unabashed delight in that younger son's return (*he
ran out to meet his son, put his arms around him, and kissed
him*) was the younger son's ability to let that delight all the
way in. The father threw a party for the younger son, and
everyone came to celebrate.

Well, almost everyone. If you're familiar with this story, the older son is usually painted in such a poor light that you can't help but hate the bastard. He seems like the kind of person who's always keeping score, and everybody owes him something. The older son was working in the fields, so the story goes, but on his way back to the house, he heard music and dancing, so he asked one of the slaves what was going on. We're led to believe he didn't even know a party had been planned at all, which sounds a little dissociative to me, but then again, I don't really blame him. Grace is a hard girl to like when she's spending all her time kissing someone else. At some point during the party, the gentle father put down his wine glass and went out to the fields to find that older son. Sometimes it takes leaving home to realize how lost you are, but sometimes it takes someone else returning home to make you realize you've *never* felt at home. When the gentle father begged the older son to come to the party, the older son did the honest thing instead of doing the right thing: he spewed out all his resentment and anger on that gentle father, soaking him with rage like water from a broken pipe.

> Sometimes it takes leaving home to realize how lost you are, but sometimes it takes someone else returning home to make you realize you've *never* felt at home.

But when you've experienced enough loss and grief without trying to fix it or numb it or deny it, you don't mind getting wet. That gentle father let that pipe run dry before saying a word. When he finally spoke, his words were aimed at the fragility hidden within that strong older son—but to hold it, not hurt it. Gentleness can penetrate the thickest of skins and pierce the hardest of hearts. "Son," he said, "you are always with me, and all I have is yours."

And that's how the story ends. We aren't told how the son responded. We don't see if his skin softened or if his heart changed. Maybe you had the kind of father who said those kinds of things to you after you poured out your anger at him, and maybe you didn't. Either way, because the story ends in mystery, it's an invitation to imagine how we might respond if our own weakness, loneliness, and fragility were met with such profound gentleness. It's also an invitation to imagine how we might welcome and befriend those parts of ourselves that, like the younger son, have wandered far from home or, like the older son, have gotten mired in the quicksand of self-righteousness. For some reason, we have a hard time treating our own weakness with anything but contempt.

Despite my undying love for Brené Brown and her groundbreaking work on the power of vulnerability, it's tempting for me to use vulnerability as a way to get people to admire me instead of as an invitation to get to know me.

Quick example: "Try/fail/learn" is a leadership mantra I love to share with anyone who will listen. The theory behind this mantra is that failure is a fantastic teacher as long as we're committed to learning from our failures. We all want to get better at what we do, but we're so afraid of failure that we rarely try anything new, which prevents us from learning anything and getting better at what we do. But one day, someone on the small team of people I lead called my bluff. I was being particularly hard on myself after making a mistake, and this person asked, "Why are you so gracious with us when we fail but so hard on yourself when you fail?"

I come by shame honestly, just like you do. Shame is how people survive. If I punish the weakest and most fragile parts of myself, perhaps they'll stay hidden so I'll never have to find out what would happen if they saw the light of day. And that's why this story that Jesus tells about the gentle father is so restorative. Shame is confronted head-on, even if twenty-first-century readers can't see it right away.

While we might admire the kind of self-sacrificial love demonstrated by the gentle father and the riches-to-rags redemption story line, first-century Palestinian listeners probably would have had a very different reaction. In a culture where family honor was the greatest currency, the lengths to which the father goes to destroy his family's honor would have turned people's stomachs. It's not the son who destroys the family's honor; that is all the father's doing. If he wouldn't have foolishly rubber-stamped his son's reckless plan in the first place, not to mention giving him back his allowance when he returned penniless and broken, we might have a story that builds moral fiber, where a soft kid learns responsibility through tough love. Instead, we're left with a story where irresponsibility is rewarded and hard work is spurned. This is not the story of a generous father; it's the story of a bighearted but weak fool.

Think about it: the younger son's demand to receive his share of the inheritance before the death of his father—and his father's willingness to give it to him—would have left an indelible mark of shame on the family's reputation, a smear that would never go away. And when that same community saw the father accept his son back and restore him to his place in the family, what little honor that might have remained would have been erased forever. Perhaps you can picture the gentle father crying when he thought he'd never see his younger son again, but can you also picture him crying over the loss of friendship he would have endured after losing his honor?

The older son was certainly angry that his younger brother was being celebrated after squandering the family's riches, but his refusal to go to the party must also have been the result of feeling too ashamed to be seen with a man who couldn't even stand up to his reckless younger son in order to restore his family's honor. Can you imagine the loneliness you'd feel if your own child saw your gift as a liability? Would it not feel like a failure if your own child looked at you not just with anger, but with sneering contempt?

I know this story is a parable and I'm reading between the lines, but remember, parables are like those Russian dolls; they include as many layers as you're willing to open. Perhaps it's easy to see the layer revealing the father's heroic, selfless compassion and unconditional love, but unless you can also peel back the layer that reveals his astounding willingness to lose everything in order to love his children, you'll only see the gentle father as a magnanimous superhero. You'll miss the wounded healer.

I'm convinced it's the father's willingness to be seen as weak that restores the younger son, who must have been broken wide open at the ridiculous glory of seeing his father running toward him in such an undignified way. I'm also convinced that the father's willingness to be seen as weak is what *prevents* restoration in the older son, who can't stand weakness or failure in himself or anyone else. If Jesus is telling us that God is like the gentle father in this story, he seems to be telling us that God doesn't mind being seen as a weak and fragile fool if it's what will unite and restore all of creation. This story, like so many of the stories Jesus tells, reveals the incarnation—the idea that an all-powerful God voluntarily became a weak, fragile, and lonely human being so that all of humanity could be restored, which of course is the pearl of great price.

Restoration doesn't come from repenting the right way (the younger son didn't), believing all the right things (you don't, and neither do I), or even welcoming our own weakness (though it's a good start). Rather, we are restored when our common humanity—our weakness, fragility, and loneliness—is received by others, sanctified by God, and befriended by ourselves.

Christians talk a lot about spiritual restoration, which is fine and necessary, but restoration starts with welcoming the weakness and fragility in our *bodies*. There are more than a few cringe-worthy doctrines within Christianity, but if I have a vote, the most cringe worthy is the dualistic nonsense that insists your spirit is good and your body is bad. Instead of shaming our bodies and silencing them, we need to learn to listen to the wisdom our bodies have to offer if we are going to be restored. Even if you've lost the will to meet God in your mind, you can often meet Her in your body, especially in those places where your body has endured pain.

Our bodies contain more than bones, ligaments, and organs; they also carry trauma. For more than thirty years, Bessel van der Kolk has worked with trauma survivors, pioneering a new field of research that suggests we store trauma in our bodies long after the traumatic event is over. When we neglect the pain in our bodies, we suffer in profound ways. But when we take the time to welcome the pain in our bodies and listen to what that pain is trying to tell us, we open ourselves up to the possibility of restoration.

When we come present to the weaknesses of our bodies and invite God to meet us in those places of pain, a deep kind of restoration is possible. The writer Alia Joy describes her journey of grief, faith, poverty, and embodiment in her book *Glorious Weakness: Discovering God in All We Lack*. It's a gritty and beautiful exploration of what it means to allow God to meet you in your body when it's at its most vulnerable—weak, instead of the strong we'd prefer it to be. Discovering God in all she lacks isn't an idea for Joy; it's a lived reality. Only seventeen teeth remain in her mouth. In addition to the difficulty of chewing food with her front teeth, she constantly fights against the stereotype that bad teeth are the result of poor life decisions. She also has bipolar disorder, and managing it requires constant readjusting of her meds, which don't always work the way they should. The medication she takes has resulted in significant weight gain. "I am a new stereotype, a new label," Joy writes. "My fat body dictates my identity for me. Society demands I apologize for being a fat woman, for the space I take up, for the choices I make, but it needs no explanation. It knows everything there is to know about me with one look. I'm not seen as a whole person, because I am a full person and a full person is automatically lazy, slow, undesirable, gross, slobby, out of control, and asexual."

Yet even though Joy feels rejected for the way her body looks and works, her body is where she has experienced God's love in the deepest way. Shortly after her book was released, she said this about how she experiences God when she's feeling particularly useless in her body: "Coming out of those areas of trauma and pain and depression and darkness, I realized that I am adored by God when I am lying in bed staring at the wall. When I am producing nothing, when I am contributing to the church in no way, when I am not out there doing a thing, I am astoundingly beloved by God." When you become aware of pain in your body, instead of fighting it, ignoring it, shaming it, or numbing it, you might ask yourself, "What if I could learn to welcome what is about my body, right here and now?" Instead of seeing pain as a nuisance, we can pay attention to it, understanding it as a gentle invitation to restoration.

· ● ● ● ·

Practice: Welcoming Weakness and Fragility in Ourselves

A body scan can be a helpful way to learn to listen to your body, so you can give it what it needs to heal. To practice a body scan, sit down or lie down comfortably in a place where you won't get interrupted. Start by bringing awareness to your breathing, and then begin to notice where your body comes into contact with the floor or the cushion of the chair on which you're sitting. Then try to notice sensations in your body; maybe there's pain in your shoulders, feet, or head. As you bring gentle focus to that area, just tune in without judging it. Don't try to figure out why you're feeling pain there; just be with it. Stay with it as long as you want to, but before moving on to a new sensation, gently release it before moving on to a new area to explore. You might release it by using a mantra, like "You are always with me, and all I have is yours," or even just a word, like *welcome*.

Your mind will wander, and that's okay. Each time it does, gently return your attention to the area of your body that hurts. The more you gently return to focus when your mind wanders, the more you'll begin to create new pathways in your brain, helping you release tension more instinctively.

The practice of using a mantra to help you create new pathways in your brain also can be helpful when you notice the ways in which you practice unkind self-talk about your body:

- When you look in the mirror and shame washes over you because you hate the shape of your body, say, "You are always with me, and all I have is yours."
- When you feel like a loser for missing an important event, like your granddaughter's birthday party, say, "You are always with me, and all I have is yours."

- When you feel like a failure because your cerebral palsy made you trip and fall again today at work, say, "You are always with me, and all I have is yours."
- When your depression returns and you feel defective, as if you'll never find the energy to do even small things, say, "You are always with me, and all I have is yours."
- When you're exhausted from burning way too many candles on way too many ends, say, "You are always with me, and all I have is yours."
- When you notice you've been dragging your body through life and it needs gentle care, say, "You are always with me, and all I have is yours."

If the mantras I suggested don't feel helpful, create your own. Whatever feels kind and welcoming will work. ●

● ● ● ● ●

Practice: Welcoming Weakness and Fragility in Others

The more you learn to be gentle with yourself, the more you're able to offer gentleness to others. Welcoming the weakness and fragility of others is like standing outside the door of someone's heart, waiting to be invited in. Once invited in, we give and receive the opportunity to feel less alone. When we find solidarity in weakness, we open ourselves up to surprising relational restoration.

The writer of the Revelation describes the Divine with surprising tenderness. "Behold," we hear God whisper, "I stand at the door, and I knock. If somebody hears me and opens the door, then I will enter."

We don't often imagine a quiet God—much less a shy God—who waits patiently behind a closed door, wondering if we hear her, wondering if we'll respond. We live in a world where people sometimes try to force their way into our hearts by cajoling, manipulating, and making empty promises. It's an exhausting and violent way to live. But God waiting for us to open the door is quiet and gentle. She wonders if she'll be invited in to see our weakness and fragility. She lingers outside the door because she hopes she'll be given an opportunity to sit with us in our pain.

Because it's so uncomfortable to see weakness and fragility in someone else, most of us are tempted to try to cover it up by offering solutions or by sharing weaknesses of our own, or even by trying to subtly change the subject. But if we can gently bear witness to someone's weakness and fragility without covering it up, a door can be opened for restoration. Maybe that's why the gentle father's response to the older son who stood outside the party in the parable is so moving. The older son wasn't ready to go in, so the gentle father patiently waited outside the door of that older son's heart, whispering, "You are always with me, and all I have is yours," not knowing if the son would ever let him in.

If you're invited to sit with someone in their pain, you might be tempted to try to do too much. Consider simply suggesting they close their eyes and invite God to see themselves in their place of pain as it really is, without editing. Allow them to have their own journey, whatever it is. Attend to them as they go inward with God. What they might see or experience isn't up to you, even if they don't see or experience anything. When they open their eyes again, and if they tell you what happened, resist the temptation to interpret it or make any connections to your own journey. If you say too much or try to relate to it too personally, you might diminish what happened in that restorative silence. If you can hold the silence by gently observing what was happening in them, you'll let them move all the way through that moment in their own time and in their own way.

Gentle, open-ended invitations can be a powerful way to welcome someone's weakness and fragility without trying to control the flow of energy. The invitation might take the form of a question:

- What are you seeing or feeling right now?
- Does this feel familiar in any way?
- What would you say or do right now if you felt completely free from all judgment?
- Where are you feeling this in your body?

Sometimes, however, simply holding someone's gaze without saying anything can create more space for them to stand in their own weakness and fragility.

Restoration is slow work, and you probably won't see much progress day by day, but then again, love doesn't demand to know how things will turn out. The gentle father responded to the older son's anger with love and acceptance, though it must have required great strength to hear his son say those hateful words and not be filled with shame. It's hard to remember that sometimes welcoming weakness and fragility in somebody else means being met with violence and anger.

I wonder if all violence can ultimately be traced to the fear of being left all alone in the world. I recently watched a movie, the culmination of three trilogies, in which a small group of freedom fighters are up against a powerful army bent on their total destruction. "They win by making you feel alone," one of them says, just before the tide turns. If that's true (and I'm convinced it is), most movies get the next bit wrong. We don't feel less alone when a magnanimous superhero saves the day. Rather, we feel at one with all of creation—we are restored—when we see someone's weakness and fragility on full display for the sake of loving and welcoming another person. The cross of Jesus the Christ is powerful not because it puts the wrath of God on display (any bully could do that), but because it reveals the weakness and fragility of God-with-us, displaying God willingly suffering indignity and shame so the whole world can join a party thrown in their honor.

"I am always with you, and all I have is yours." A person who has received their own weakness, fragility, and loneliness with gentleness can give away that much without losing a thing. The heart is the place where we meet others, suffer, and rejoice with them. It is the place where we can identify and be in solidarity with them. Whenever we love, we are not alone. Whenever we love, we are at one with all of creation, standing at the corner of Fourth and Walnut with Thomas Merton, where we can see the secret beauty and depth of each and every heart, where neither sin nor desire nor self-knowledge can reach. Standing in that place, we can see and be seen with God's eyes, as we truly are. ●

●   ●   ●   ●   ●

How Love Grows

Often I wish my enemies and
those who try to hurt me an

equal harm, like to like—as
anger meets anger and hate

meets hate—but You keep
reminding me, early and late,

that love is unlike meeting like.

FINDING GOD WHEREVER YOU GO

Because Thomas Merton's writings continue to affect countless people from many faith traditions, you might think his life had always shone like the sun. But given the tragic losses he suffered as a child and the consistent failure he experienced as a young adult, it's surprising he ever wrote anything or went anywhere. Before becoming one of the most influential contemplative voices of our time, Merton was just a cynical, failed novelist.

His mother died when he was six. His father died of a brain tumor just ten years later. His older brother was killed during an air battle over the English Channel in 1943. In his early twenties, feeling a strong desire to become a priest, he approached the Franciscans, who convinced him—apparently without subtlety—that he didn't have a vocational call. When his dream of being a priest evaporated, he became an English teacher, finishing three novels in two years; none of them were accepted for publication. After giving up writing (*and apparently giving away all of his clothing*), he found himself on the doorsteps of Gethsemane at age twenty-six, committed to joining the Trappists. He stayed there until he died at age fifty-three after being electrocuted when he came into contact with a fan with bad wiring.

Between ages twenty-six and fifty-three, Thomas Merton rarely left Gethsemane. The only time he ever really traveled was in 1968, when he received permission to go to Asia to visit Buddhist monasteries and meet with the Dalai Lama. But if there was ever a human being who got where he needed to go by learning to be where he was, it was Thomas Merton. If there was ever a person who learned to stand in a place long enough to see who he really was, it was Thomas Merton.

Henri Nouwen describes Merton as having "an intense personality, which registered with a maximum sensitivity everything that he read, saw, and experienced, always posing the question as large as life itself: What can I say 'yes' to, without reserve?" He found his yes by learning to befriend silence and solitude. Merton began learning to pray using *The Spiritual Exercises* by Ignatius of Loyola, though he apparently was afraid that doing the exercises would "plunge him head-first into mysticism before he was aware of it." (*Hello, slippery slope. You'll end up leading us all the way back home if we can keep our eyes open all the way down.*)

Soon Merton found himself at ease sitting cross-legged for long periods of time in the mornings, simply staring at a crucifix. He became less tense, less agitated, less needy, and less restless, and the beauty of nature around him consistently left him awestruck with wonder. Yet he sustained a clear-eyed consciousness about the world, especially as World War II was breaking out. He was forced to consider how he might be a person of peace in a world of war. Because Merton had learned by practicing silence and solitude to detach from chaotic thoughts, which stole his peace away, he became a person of peace by learning to detach from the illusion that he owned anything, even his life. Because he saw himself as having literally nothing to defend, he found that he could move straight into the center of violence and evil and destroy it.

Merton became one of the most important writers on nonviolence, quoting Gandhi often. He seemed to see the best of Christianity, like practicing nonviolence through the way of Jesus, and the best of Buddhism, like detachment and self-emptying, as complementary rather than contradictory. "It becomes overwhelmingly important for us to become detached from our everyday conception of ourselves as potential subjects for special and unique experience," Merton wrote in his book *Mystics and Zen Masters,* which was published posthumously in 1969. "This means that a spiritual guide worth his salt will conduct a ruthless campaign against all forms of delusion arising out of spiritual ambition and self-complacency which aim to establish the ego in spiritual glory. . . . That is why the Zen Masters say: 'If you meet the Buddha, kill him.'"

In case that feels a little dense, Jim Carrey, the hilarious actor with the rubber face who gave the world Ace Ventura *and* Lloyd Christmas, thanks be to God, can add to the conversation. He once said he wished everyone could get rich and famous and get everything they wanted, so they could see that it's not the answer. It's a sound bite people like to quote often, but I think it leaves us on the outside looking in without the bigger context. The quote comes from an interview in which Carrey gets remarkably honest about his own journey of letting go of ego. Here's a bit more:

> "I believe that I had to become a famous idea and accomplish a bunch of things that look like success in order to give up my attachment to those things. It's been part of the evolution of ego is to spend the first half of your life acquiring and adding, thinking you can add to yourself. . . but that can never fulfill you. Wholeness is a different feeling than me-ness. They're all characters that I played. Jim Carrey was a less intentional character because I thought I was just building something that people would like, but it was a character. I played the character of a guy who was free from concerns so that people who watched me would be free from concern. Depression is your body saying, *fuck you*, I don't want to be this character anymore. I don't want to hold up this avatar that you've created in the world, it's too much for me. You can think of

the word depressed as deep rest. Your body needs deep rest from the character you've been trying to play."

Thomas Merton was right: the ego only knows how to run a campaign for personal spiritual glory. Jim Carrey is right, too: wholeness *is* a different feeling than me-ness. Both men learned to walk away from their script and return to ordinariness. When we can let go of our false self, or our script, we are free from the responsibility to create—and then destroy—new universes in which we are the center, which is exhausting work.

The journey that leads us to give up our campaign for personal spiritual glory, abandoning me-ness for wholeness, is so universally human that it shows up in every religion and every culture across every generation. Joseph Campbell called it the hero's journey. Campbell, a comparative mythologist who studied the similarities of cultural myths and religious stories during a time when everyone else was studying the differences, discovered what he called a monomyth—a basic story pattern found in many narratives from around the world—he referred to as the hero's journey. This story structure, seen in nearly all religions and cultures, involves three basic stages: a departure, an invitation, and eventually a return. The hero's journey forms the structure of our favorite stories, including *Star Wars*, the Harry Potter series, *The Lord of the Rings*—and the Gospels, too.

Here's how the hero's journey goes. The hero lives in the ordinary world (*Luke Skywalker on Tatooine, Harry Potter at*

4 Privet Drive, Frodo in the Shire) until they receive an invitation to leave. When they finally do leave, there's no turning back, and they meet enemies who test them, friends who walk with them, and mentors who teach them. Finally, the hero faces a supreme test, which requires all their skills and resources to overcome and will also force them to face an inner conflict: Will they reinforce their own ego, or will they sacrifice their ego for the good of the many? If they overcome the supreme test and choose to relinquish ego, they can return home, bearing gifts for the good of the people who live there.

If we see the story of the gentle father and his two sons through the lens of a fairy tale, the leather-clad bad boy turns into the respectable prince because of a gentle father's kiss. That's a sweet story (*unless you're married to the older son*), but it's not all that interesting. The younger son is now just a respectable prince who wears the royal ring while enjoying parties. *Borrring.* Is that really the end of anyone's story?

If we see the story of Jacob and Esau through the lens of a fairy tale, we might try to see Jacob's journey as a formula. We might be tempted to sleep under the stars with a rock for a pillow and wait for God to speak to us the same way God spoke to Jacob. But that would turn God into a predictable vending machine.

But if we can see those stories through the lens of the hero's journey, they can keep teaching us as we discern our own departures, receive our own invitations, and return home again after our perilous adventures. The younger son left and returned. The older son never left but received an invitation. Jacob met God in a dream, and what God said to him essentially outlined the hero's journey in a sentence: "I will be with you and keep you wherever you go and will bring you back to this land; for I will not leave you until I have done what I have promised you." If those stories follow the structure of a monomyth, each time we read them we can ask ourselves new questions, like this:

What am I being asked to leave . . .

to search for something, . . .

which will test my character . . .

and introduce me to wily enemies, wise mentors, and trustworthy companions, . . .

who will help me see my weakness and fragility and invite me to develop strength and resilience . . .

and lead me to my own supreme test, which will require all my skill and all my resources to overcome it, . . .

so I can return back home with gifts to give and good news to share?

True to any real hero's journey, Jacob's life had anything but a fairy-tale ending. Soon after meeting God in that dream, he fell in love with his cousin Rachel and married her (*it's complicated*), but only after marrying Rachel's older sister, Leah, having been tricked by Jacob's devious uncle, Laban. Jacob got revenge by swindling Laban out of all of his strong animals and by becoming an extremely wealthy man—which, for the record, doesn't make you a hero, then or now. Jacob and Laban eventually reconciled (*after a fashion*), and soon afterward, without any record in the Bible as to why he did it, Jacob took all of his family and all of his cattle and headed toward his childhood home in an attempt to make peace with his twin brother, Esau, whom he had wronged all those years ago—which, for the record, does make you a hero, then and now.

When Esau heard about Jacob's impending arrival, he headed out to meet his twin—with four hundred soldiers, armed to the teeth. Jacob had indeed returned "back to this land," just as God had said he would, but apparently, he returned to die. Terrified, Jacob sent half of his family and animals out to meet Esau (*the hero is sometimes a coward first*) and spent what he suspected would be his last night on earth alone. Only he was not alone; Jacob wrestled with a man until dawn, fiercely hanging onto him until he received the blessing he'd longed for his whole life. He walked away with a lifetime limp, but he got that blessing in the form of a new name: Israel, which means "he who wrestles with God and humanity and prevails." Jacob and Esau reconciled the next day, with tears of joy.

Jacob's life is ignominious, to be sure, but it's also heroic, because he kept wrestling; he kept returning to here. Israel's life teaches us that it really is glorious to wrestle with God until you receive what you've always longed for, despite a million wrong turns, deceptions, and bad choices. To wrestle with God is to keep returning to here until you find what you're looking for.

On your own hero's journey, you'll feel like a bumbling idiot most of the time. You'll resist invitations to leave, you'll betray friends who only wanted to help, and you'll falter when you face your deep inner conflict. The hero always resists the invitation to leave home at first. But eventually, you'll let go of that trapeze, because there really are things you still want from God, and that really is one of the most glorious things about you. And when you do, you'll find God eternally waiting for you with love in that moment, before you grab onto anything else.

Mindfulness isn't just about breathing, and it isn't just about learning to do what you are doing. It's the journey of waking up to—and participating with—the new creation that each moment offers. Practicing mindfulness will take us somewhere. The more we detach from the ego's self-important agenda, the more we will find God wherever we go.

- Practicing *attentiveness* is learning to return to Here so you can find God waiting for you with love in the eternal Now.
- Practicing *ordinariness* is learning to return to who you are and away from who you think you should be.
- Practicing *simplicity* is learning to give unambiguous yeses and unapologetic noes in ways that leave margin and space.
- Practicing *rhythm* is learning to hear and play your part in the song the universe is singing.
- Practicing *conversation* is learning to ask questions that continually expand how you see and understand the world.
- Practicing *delight* is learning to fully receive whatever is in front of you.
- Practicing *restoration* is learning to welcome the weakness, fragility, and loneliness in yourself and others for mutual healing.

You are going somewhere, and God is smiling. God is with you and for you in every moment of your life. May you find God wherever you are, with laughter and tears and starstruck wonder. And may you find God wherever you go, with fear and trembling, while stumbling and falling and getting back up again.

And if Thomas Merton was wrong, if there really *is* a way to tell people that they are all walking around shining like the sun, may you discover how to tell them.

· ● · ·

Then

If I could
trust that
You are enough
I would know
that I am
enough.

GRATITUDE

A mindful life leads to an awareness of the special people who offer help, support, friendship, encouragement and inspiration necessary for a project like this to come together. When I think about the experience of writing this book, these are some of the people for whom I feel the most gratitude:

Tony Jones convinced me to ditch my original idea for this one, which turned out to be far superior. Thank you for seeing more and pressing in.

Chris Ferebee is my agent who has been with me since my first book. Thank you for constantly reminding me that I'm building something and it's worth it.

Lil Copan is my brilliant editor who taught me how to be a writer of books and not just a writer of sentences. Thank you for coaxing so much more out of this book than was there at first.

The rest of the team at Fortress Press in Minneapolis: Allyce Amidon and Karen Schenkenfelder for their superior copyediting; Layne Johnson for her steady project management; James Kegley for his beautiful and creative design support; Jill Braithwaite for giving the green light to this project in the first place; and especially for Alison Vandenberg, Senior Director of Marketing, for enduring my endless title revisions with patience and grace.

Kevin van der Leek designed the gorgeous cover. Thank you for getting it just right.

Ed Cyzewski provided expert advice and many helpful suggestions for helping me incorporate mindful practices that actually are mindful and are actually practices. Thank you for being a contemplative soul in a just-get-on-with-it world.

Brandi Carlile's gorgeous melodies and honest lyrics provided the soundtrack for nearly every page. Thank you for nourishing my soul as I bled on the page.

Will and Charlie and Chad: thank you for so much unconditional love, the nonjudgmental support and the raucous laughter. Can't imagine these last two years without you three.

Becky and Rick Patton are our Sunday night friends who let us be ourselves and who taught us how to share a table. Thank you for the priceless gift of being cherished.

Our parents: Harold and Claudia, and Pat; Our siblings Joel and Kathy, Adam and Susie, Dave and Julie, Lisa and Jeff; Our nephews and nieces Ella, Brody, Evan, Carly, Olivia, Sophia, Halle and Maggie. Thank you for being the circle of love that reminds us there's no outside of inside.

My boys: Isaac, Elijah, and Ben. Thank you for making me laugh so hard.

My wife Mary edited my first draft with honesty and kindness. Thank you for believing in who I am and also in who I am becoming. Thank you also for enduring a much longer process than either of us anticipated.

And finally, my father-in-law, James M. Martin, who died before this book went to print. Thank you for loving me from the moment I met you standing in front of that broken closet door at your house in Plymouth to your last breath. You accepted me just as I am, despite our disagreements. I'd be honored if you'd come and meet me when it's my time, and I'll be disappointed if you didn't bring a book for me to read.

NOTES

Finding God Where You Are

There's an ancient story in which God, having recently created human beings, realized that a terrible mistake had been made.

When I first read the story about God attempting to avoid our incessant claptrap by choosing to hide within us, I laughed out loud. I generally prefer the *idea* of searching for God to the reality of shining the flashlight into the murky depths of my unfamiliar soul. Yet whenever I've drummed up enough courage to go there, I eventually do find her there. The story I retell appears in the chapter entitled "Svadhyaya" in Deborah Adele, *Yamas and Niyamas* (Duluth, MN: On-Ward Bound, 2009), Kindle location 1515. I reworked some of the language.

It drove most people crazy, but Jesus talked about finding God using mostly paradoxical language . . .

Jesus was a master at using paradox to keep people searching for God instead of settling for a god that was too small. "Those who find their life will lose it, and those who lose their life for my sake will find it" (Matthew 10:39, NRSV); "Whoever loves father or mother more than me is not worthy of me; and whoever loves son or daughter more than me is not worthy of me" (Matthew 10:37, NRSV); "The kingdom of heaven is like treasure hidden in a field, which someone found and hid; then in his joy he goes and sells all that he has and buys that field" (Matthew 13:44, NRSV).

Here and Now

> Jon M. Sweeney and Mark S. Burrows, *Meister Eckhart's Book of the Heart: Meditations for the Restless Soul* (Charlottesville: Hampton Roads, 2017), 162.

A story is told about a time Saint Francis of Assisi couldn't find God anywhere.

> Legend has it that Saint Francis had this exchange with the almond tree, but of course, it can't be proved. (https://www.franciscanmedia.org/celebrating-saint-francis-of-assisi). "'Speak to me of God.' And the almond tree blossomed" is also attributed to Nikos Kazantzakis in *The Fratricides* (New York: Simon and Schuster, 1964).

In the story of Esau and Jacob . . .

> The story of Jacob and Esau (in Genesis 25–28) is complicated, because every person is caricatured: Isaac is blind, Rebecca is cunning, Esau is stupid, Jacob is manipulative, and everybody plays their part perfectly. But when Rebecca notices how much the twins are fighting within her womb, God lets her in on a secret: two peoples are within you, and one will be stronger than the other, and the older will serve the younger (Genesis 25:21–26). Who can live with that kind of secret? And does it refer to what will happen, what could happen, or even what should happen? I've always thought of Rebecca as aiding and abetting Jacob by urging him to deceive his father, but what if she is simply trying to follow what God told her?

One day, the modern mystic Thomas Merton was out running errands . . .

> Thomas Merton, *Conjectures of a Guilty Bystander* (Garden City, NY: Doubleday, 1966), 153–54.

Ever Shining Light

> Jon M. Sweeney and Mark S. Burrows, *Meister Eckhart's Book of the Heart: Meditations for the Restless Soul* (Charlottesville: Hampton Roads, 2017), 172.

Practice 1: Attentiveness

Using the metaphor of a person trapped inside a phone booth while frantically swatting at a bee . . .

> Martin Laird talks about the reactive mind in *An Ocean of Light: Contemplation, Transformation, and Liberation* (New York:

Oxford University Press, 2018), a helpful book that encourages people to learn to cultivate a receptive mind through the practice of silence and contemplative prayer. My friend Ed Cyzewski, who introduced me to that book, wrote a short blog post about the receptive mind versus the reactive mind, including this gem: "Over time we can train ourselves to become quiet, to resist the urge to react, and to eventually meet the highs and lows of life with more awareness and stability. We can learn to receive what God is doing in our days without having to react in any particular way." You can read the rest of Ed's post at "The Struggle to Pray with a Reactive Mind in a Social Media Society," *This Kinda Contemplative Life* (blog), April 19, 2019, https://bit.ly /2lwN3Ch.

If you swipe left on a Tinder bio . . .

This is an actual Tinder profile of a thirty-three-year-old guy named James. In his profile picture, he is dragging hard on a cigarette while staring wildly off camera as if he has suddenly realized he's being robbed at gunpoint.

"For things to be revealed to us," Thich Nhat Hanh observed . . .

Thich Nhat Hanh, *Being Peace* (Berkeley, CA: Parallax, 2005), 50.

What if we stopped forcing the Bible to be divine historical journalism and started looking for the differences between true stories and truth stories?

I am borrowing from Rabbi Sandy Sasso when I differentiate between "true stories and truth stories." I first heard her use this phrase at the Festival for Faith and Writing in 2018, and it opened up a whole new way of untangling the knot of what's literally true in the Bible and what's not without losing Truth. Here's how she explains it: "When I talk about religion and stories, often kids say, 'Is that story true? Did that really happen?' I make a distinction between *true* stories and *truth* stories. And I say that some of the stories may not be true in the sense that we can actually document that these events happened, or these people lived, but they are *truth* stories that teach us something about human nature and the world. You know, children are really able to deal with that. I've seen that when I talk to kids. They say, 'Oh, I get it.' But when they grow up, they grow out of it." "Sandy Sasso: Experiencing

Religion through Story," Faith & Leadership, December 1, 2014, https://tinyurl.com/yyrzyadv.

Paradoxically, the first time the word love *is mentioned in the Bible . . .*
This story, found in Genesis 22, remains one of the most intriguing, beguiling stories in all of the Scriptures, especially considering how little we are told about the rest of Isaac's life.

Start by take a deep breath in, let it out, set a timer for five minutes . . .
Regarding setting a timer for silence, sometimes you really do forget to set one. I get together once a month with a few people to talk about our secrets without giving each other advice. We usually begin with ten minutes of silence, which feels like an eternity anyway, but once the guy who usually sets the timer really did forget. One by one, we started opening our eyes and raising our eyebrows, and then we laughed our heads off.

The following suggestions for entering into contemplative prayer are adapted from Father Thomas Keating's four movements to centering prayer.
Father Thomas Keating was dismayed that many people left Christianity in the 1960s to pursue meditation outside of Christianity, so he began to teach people how to meditate using centering prayer and other methods of contemplative prayer. You can learn more about centering prayer in many of his writings, but I recommend starting with *Open Mind, Open Heart,* 20th anniversary ed. (New York: Bloomsbury Continuum, 2019).

We Must Abandon God
Jon M. Sweeney and Mark S. Burrows, *Meister Eckhart's Book of the Heart: Meditations for the Restless Soul* (Charlottesville: Hampton Roads, 2017), 59.

Practice 2: Ordinariness

In the pilot, he follows one of his marks into an acting class . . .
B. Hader, dir., "Chapter One: Make Your Mark," *Barry,* aired March 25, 2018, on HBO.

Father Thomas Keating understood the architecture of our scripts, or false selves, as our "program for happiness."
At times, Father Keating can be a little dense, but his theory on why we created the script we now follow is so helpful. You cannot

change your script if you're not aware of why you're following it in the first place. The discussion in the text is from Thomas Keating, *The Human Condition: Contemplation and Transformation* (New York: Paulist, 1999), 9–10.

In the middle of the second season, Barry finds himself at Cousineau's apartment . . .

L. Johnson, dir. "What?!," *Barry*, aired April 21, 2019, on HBO.

Within Me in That Soft Place

Jon M. Sweeney and Mark S. Burrows, *Meister Eckhart's Book of the Heart: Meditations for the Restless Soul* (Charlottesville: Hampton Roads, 2017), 99.

Practice 3: Simplicity

It lets me listen to podcasts on limitless subjects . . .

On the subject of podcasts, I have one. It's called *This Good Word with Steve Wiens: Reclaiming What's Holy about our Humanity* (www.thisgoodword.podbean.com). It's over two hundred episodes strong, and it's one of my favorite creative outlets.

One night, after a long day surrounded by people and their needs, Jesus climbed into a boat . . .

The story of Jesus calming the storm is found in three of the four gospels: Mark 4:35–41; Matthew 8:23–27; Luke 8:22–25. The disciples were seasoned fishermen but thought they were going to die, so it must have been quite a storm. Also, this is one of those stories that may leave you scratching your head. If it does, remember Rabbi Sandi Sasso, who said there are *true* stories and there are *truth* stories. Even if you can't buy the miracle part of this story, you can see that Jesus knew something true about simplicity if he could sleep through a storm that had seasoned fishermen essentially asking for last rites.

"Everything that pretends to be a matter of life and death . . ."

Paula D'Arcy, "Is There Life after Death?," *U.S. Catholic*, January 2006, available at https://bit.ly/2T6LWWH. My wife, Mary, introduced me to Paula D'Arcy many years ago, and D'Arcy has been one of my mentors from afar ever since. She has written ten books, but you should start with *Gift of the Red Bird* (New York: Crossroad, 2002). Paula also founded the Red Bird Foundation, where she teaches, leads retreats and workshops, and helps people process deep grief.

Paula D'Arcy says that the defining, unchanging dedication of the Red Bird Foundation is . . .
Red Bird Foundation website, http://www.redbirdfoundation.com/foundation.

Immediately after Jesus calmed the storm . . .
This odd story, found in Mark 5:1–20, shows Jesus's unique ability to not only sleep in the storm but also see a human being in need when everybody else could see only death. I don't quite know what to make of Jesus casting demons out of a person and sending them into a herd of pigs, but I give this story high marks for a dramatic ending.

Your Single Yes of Love
Jon M. Sweeney and Mark S. Burrows, *Meister Eckhart's Book of the Heart: Meditations for the Restless Soul* (Charlottesville: Hampton Roads, 2017), 173.

Practice 4: Rhythm

In What Is My Song?, *their retelling of a traditional African fable . . .*
Dennis Linn, Sheila Fabricant Linn, and Matthew Linn, *What Is My Song?* (Mahwah, NJ: Paulist, 2018).

Gail Honeyman gives us tantalizing threads to pull . . .
Gail Honeyman, *Eleanor Oliphant Is Completely Fine* (New York: Pamela Dorman, 2017). Please do yourself a favor and read this hilarious and tender book. Even better, listen to it; it's magnificently narrated by Cathleen McCarron.

But that pain isn't the only true thing about him, and it doesn't have to be the defining sentence of the story he's now writing.
In Pádraig Ó Tuama's brilliant book *In the Shelter: Finding a Home in the World* (London: Hodder & Stoughton, 2015), he tells of a question he asks people on his travels: "If, right now, you were to tell the story of your life, what would the first sentence be?" Ó Tuama, my favorite poet from the north of Ireland, writes, leads retreats, and speaks extensively. When he works with groups of people, he frequently asks them the same question. It's his way

of helping them remember their song—something he has spent many years doing himself.

In an interview with Krista Tippett, Remen said . . .
Rachel Naomi Remen has the kind of voice that makes you melt. She's gentle, wise, and unpretentious. This quote comes from an interview with Krista Tippett on the *On Being* podcast. Krista Tippett, "Rachel Naomi Remen: The Difference between Fixing and Healing," *On Being* (American Public Media), originally published August 11, 2005, republished November 22, 2018, https://onbeing.org/programs/rachel-naomi-remen-the-difference-between-fixing-and-healing-nov2018.

A few years ago, I attended a lecture given by Jim Bear Jacobs . . .
Jim Bear Jacobs is a spellbinding, wise teacher. If you have not spent time listening to Native Americans talk about spirituality, you have not heard the whole story. The lecture I heard was not recorded, but you can hear a similar version at "Stories from Genesis 1," Church of All Nations, Columbia Heights, Minnesota, April 27, 2014, audio recording, https://www.cando.org/sermons/stories-from-genesis-chapter-1.

Thich Nhat Hanh wrote, "This is exactly what Jesus was trying to overcome . . ."
Thich Nhat Hanh became dear friends with Thomas Merton, which helps explain this surprising quote. It's from *Living Buddha, Living Christ* (New York: Riverhead, 1995), 31, which is a great place to start if you are hungry to find resources that combine rather than separate the wisdom traditions of the East and West.

Study the Stone
Jon M. Sweeney and Mark S. Burrows, *Meister Eckhart's Book of the Heart: Meditations for the Restless Soul* (Charlottesville: Hampton Roads, 2017), 26.

Practice 5: Conversation

In Conjectures of a Guilty Bystander, *Thomas Merton writes about the universal human desire to possess "the truth."*
Thomas Merton, *Conjectures of a Guilty Bystander* (New York: Image, 1965), 72–73.

The first five jewels (the Yamas) . . .

If you'd like to explore the Yamas and Niyamas further, read Deborah Adele, *The Yamas and Niyamas: Exploring Yoga's Ethical Practice* (Duluth, MN: On-Ward Bound, 2009).

Jesus said it this way: Love your enemies, pray for those who curse you.

Many practitioners of nonviolence—including Gandhi, Bishop Oscar Romero, and Dr. Martin Luther King Jr.—were inspired by the teachings of Jesus, particularly regarding how to respond to an enemy. "You have heard that it was said, 'You shall love your neighbor and hate your enemy.' But I say to you, Love your enemies and pray for those who persecute you." (Matthew 5:43–44, NRSV).

The parable of the Good Samaritan is a good example of the kinds of questions Jesus asked . . .

The parable of the Good Samaritan can be found in Luke 10:25–37.

One of the books we read was Zen and the Art of Motorcycle Maintenance *by Robert Pirsig.*

Robert M. Pirsig, *Zen and the Art of Motorcycle Maintenance*, Kindle ed. (New York: HarperCollins e-books, 1976). Here is the original quote from page 288:

> Because we're unaccustomed to it, we don't usually see that there's a third possible logical term equal to yes and no which is capable of expanding our understanding in an unrecognized direction. We don't even have a term for it, so I'll have to use the Japanese mu. Mu means "no thing." Like "Quality" it points outside the process of dualistic discrimination. Mu simply says, "No class; not one, not zero, not yes, not no." It states that the context of the question is such that a yes or no answer is in error and should not be given. "Unask the question" is what it says.

Mu *was reincarnated for me when recently I listened to a podcast featuring Pádraig Ó Tuama . . .*

You can listen to the *On Being* episode where Krista Tippett interviews Pádraig Ó Tuama, or you can read the manuscript here:

"Belonging Creates and Undoes Us," *On Being*, aired March 2, 2017, last updated April 11, 2019, https://bit.ly/2G5fCNU.
Behind You
Jon M. Sweeney and Mark S. Burrows, *Meister Eckhart's Book of the Heart: Meditations for the Restless Soul* (Charlottesville: Hampton Roads, 2017), 69.

Practice 6: Delight

Lenny Duncan describes his own kairos *moment . . .*
Lenny Duncan, *Dear Church: A Love Letter from a Black Preacher to the Whitest Denomination in the U.S.* (Minneapolis: Fortress Press, 2019), 1.
Thich Nhat Hanh addresses this in his classic book, The Miracle of Mindfulness, *where he writes, "All time is my time."*
Thich Nhat Hanh, *The Miracle of Mindfulness*, trans. Mobi Ho (Boston: Beacon, 1975).
Rabbi Abraham Joshua Heschel understood time as holy.
Abraham Joshua Heschel, *The Sabbath*, FSG Classics, Kindle ed. (New York: Farrar, Straus & Giroux, 1951). The Hebrew word for holy is *kadosh*, which shows up first in Genesis 2:3, on the seventh day of creation, when God rests after all the work of creating that God did: "So God blessed the seventh day and hallowed it, because on it God rested from all the work that he had done in creation" (Genesis 2:3).
"Every instant is an act of creation,"
Heschel, *The Sabbath*.
Your Only Delight
Jon M. Sweeney and Mark S. Burrows, *Meister Eckhart's Book of the Heart: Meditations for the Restless Soul* (Charlottesville: Hampton Roads, 2017), 129.

Practice 7: Restoration

Jesus once told a story about a gentle father who had two sons . . .
The story, typically referred to as the parable of the Prodigal Son, can be read in Luke 15:11–32.

For more than thirty years, Bessel van der Kolk has worked with trauma survivors . . .

Bessel van der Kolk is a pioneering researcher who has spent over thirty years working with trauma survivors, helping them find healing for their horrific losses. He uses scientific advances to show how trauma reshapes our bodies and our brains, compromising our ability to experience pleasure, exercise self-control, and trust ourselves and others. Read more in his book *The Body Keeps the Score: Brain, Mind, and Body in the Healing of Trauma* (New York: Viking, 2014).

"I am a new stereotype, a new label," Joy writes.

Alia Joy, *Glorious Weakness: Discovering God in All We Lack*, Kindle ed. (Grand Rapids: Baker, 2019). I loved reading Joy's book and interviewing her for my podcast. She writes and speaks with a refreshing honesty that welcomes fragility because she'd die if she didn't.

"Coming out of those areas of trauma and pain and depression and darkness . . .

This quote comes from a podcast interview I did with Alia Joy. "Glorious Weakness with Alia Joy," *This Good Word with Steve Wiens*, episode 179, April 11, 2019, podcast, https://thisgood word.podbean.com/e/episode-179-glorious-weakness-with -alia-joy.

A body scan can be a helpful way to learn to listen to your body . . .

Body scans are a great way to welcome weakness and fragility in a gentle, nonjudgmental way. Many resources are available to guide you through a body scan meditation. You can spend as little as three to five minutes with it or as much as thirty to forty minutes, depending on what works for you. A great place to start is Elaine Smookler, "Beginner's Body Scan Meditation," *Mindful*, April 11, 2019, https://tinyurl.com/ycasdoam.

The writer of the Revelation describes the Divine with surprising tenderness. "Listen," we hear God whisper, "I am standing at the door and knocking; if you hear my voice and open the door, I will come in to you and eat with you, and you with me."

Revelation 3:27, NRSV.

They win by making you feel alone . . .
>   J. J. Abrams, dir., *Star Wars, Episode IX: The Rise of Skywalker*
>   (Los Angeles: Walt Disney Pictures, 2019).

How Love Grows
>   Jon M. Sweeney and Mark S. Burrows, *Meister Eckhart's Book of
>   the Heart: Meditations for the Restless Soul* (Charlottesville: Hamp-
>   ton Roads, 2017), 78.

Finding God Wherever You Go

Henri Nouwen describes Merton as having "an intense personality . . ."
>   Henri Nouwen, *Thomas Merton: Contemplative Critic* (New York:
>   Triumph, 1991), originally published as *Pray to Live*, 19.

Merton began learning to pray using The Spiritual Exercises *by Ignatius of Loyola, though he apparently was afraid that doing the
exercises would "plunge him head-first into mysticism before he was
aware of it."*
>   Nouwen, *Thomas Merton: Contemplative Critic*, 22.

*"It becomes overwhelmingly important for us to become detached from
our everyday conception of ourselves as potential subjects for special
and unique experience,"*
>   Thomas Merton, *Mystics and Zen Masters* (New York: Farrar,
>   Straus & Giroux, 1967), 76–77. Merton published sixty-one
>   books, which is prolific against any standard. Where do you start?
>   If you're interested in the Merton writings that include his most
>   advanced thinking on East meeting West, you might want to start
>   with *Mystics and Zen Masters*.

*"I believe that I had to become a famous idea and accomplish a bunch of
things . . ."*
>   The Jim Carrey quote comes from an interview in which Carrey
>   gets remarkably honest about his journey of detaching from what
>   he thought would bring him happiness. I was especially intrigued
>   by how he talked about realizing that the pursuit of "me" was
>   just another role he played. You can watch the interview here:
>   "Jim Carrey: What It All Means|One of the Most Eye Opening
>   Speeches," YouTube video, 5:44, uploaded by Absolute Motiva-
>   tion, November 4, 2017, https://bit.ly/2Z9kcXz=.

Joseph Campbell called it the hero's journey.

To learn more about the twelve stages of the hero's journey, see Joseph Campbell, *The Hero with a Thousand Faces*, 3rd ed. (Novato, CA: New World Library, 2008).

"I will be with you and keep you wherever you go and will bring you back to this land; for I will not leave you until I have done what I have promised you."

Genesis 28:15.

Then

Jon M. Sweeney and Mark S. Burrows, *Meister Eckhart's Book of the Heart: Meditations for the Restless Soul* (Charlottesville: Hampton Roads, 2017), 198.